Mel Bay Presents

ENCYCLOPEDIA
of
Guitar Chord Inversions

by Brian Balthazor

LONGWOOD PUBLIC LIBRARY

1 2 3 4 5 6 7 8 9 0

Visit us on the Web at www.melbay.com — E-mail us at email@melbay.com

1.0 Preface

Years ago I walked into a jazz club in La Jolla, California and was amazed at the music coming from the instrumentalist on stage. The guitarist sat with eyes closed, intimately in touch with the music, instrument, and surroundings. In addition to a complete mastery of the single line jazz solo, Peter Sprague was equally skilled at chord soloing where entire songs were effortlessly played throughout the fretboard using chords with proper voice leading.

Later as a student, it soon became apparent how this level of mastery was attained. Employing music theory, chord construction, and subdividing the guitar into conquerable zones, it was demonstrated how to play virtually any chord on the guitar with different chord densities and voicings in any key. The guitar chord inversion system was explained to me verbally, though the task of mapping out the myriad chord voicings was heretofore incomplete.

The book title "Encyclopedia of Guitar Chord Inversions" is a misnomer, as this book more precisely describes a "Guitar Chord Inversion System" based on music theory and a few base chord patterns which allow you to generate thousands of chords. If properly understood, this "Encyclopedia" will be internalized and rendered a mere bookshelf reference. Which should be your personal goal.

If you do not read music, this book can be of assistance – though I suggest obtaining a good instructor to fill in the gaps in your knowledge and provide further inspiration. The first few sections are dense and should be understood to derive the full benefit of the chord diagrams which follow in the later sections. Give these sections adequate time.

The process of creating this book took nine years from conception to publishing. I'm passing the baton to you to spend one year to put it into practice. My reward will hopefully be some good listening download. Send me book suggestions and/or music clips to brianb@kauai.com

Brian Balthazor

July, 2006

2.0 Credits

Thanks to Peter Sprague for his artistry, knowledge, time, tips, and input during the process. The kinship we share is among my cherished possessions. Thanks also to his wife Stephanie for the kind editorial assistance.

A very special thanks to my wife Victoria, for unselfishly giving herself and time while I wrote this book, nurturing our three children and being a true friend.

Thanks to Bette Goodrich for sharing her being; a woman of wisdom, spirit, and soul that recently unravelled the final mystery of life. She will be missed, but not forgotten.

I wish to thank my parents Audrey and William for the many sacrifices made in my name. Though their time on earth was short, the impact is still being felt.

I am extremely thankful for the thoughtful courtesy and professionalism exhibited by those at Mel Bay Publications including Sheri Schleusner, Rachel Cooper, Mig Gianino, Shawnna Troxel, Karen Dean, Julie Price, Doug Falloon, Bill Bay, and others I might have missed.

3.0 Introduction

This book defines a movable guitar chord system in standard guitar "E" tuning. The material is directed toward the student, though it can be used as a reference once familiar with the material.

Chords in Section 5.1 "Low Density Series" display the chord note and function (root, third, fifth, seventh, etc.). Later sections display the chord pattern, though omit exact fingering.

4.0. Chord Theory

Three main chord families exist:

1. Major

2. Minor

3. Dominant

4.1 Major Chord Family

Figure 1 displays the C major scale, a seven tone scale void of accidentals.

Figure 1. C Major Scale

Figure 2 displays the C Major triad and $C^{\Delta 7}$ chords respectively.

Figure 2. C Major And C Major 7 Chords

Major chords can be altered by raising or lowering the fifth (♭5, #5), or adding a major 9. In addition, a sixth can be added to the major triad to form a major 6th, which can also be altered by adding a major 9. Figure 3 contains the complete list of major chords studied in this text in the key of C.

Figure 3. C Major Chord Family

Figure 4 displays the C Dorian minor scale, a seven tone scale containing a ♭3 and ♭7. A variety of other minor scales exist, though we limit our discussion to the Dorian minor scale.

Figure 4. C Dorian Minor Scale

Figure 5 displays the C minor triad and Cmin7 chords respectively.

Figure 5. C Minor and C Minor 7 Chords

Minor chords can be altered by raising or lowering the fifth (♭5, #5), or adding a major 9 (similar to major chords). The sixth can also be used in place of the ♭7 to yield a minor sixth chord, which can be altered by adding a ninth. You can also use the major seventh in place of the ♭7. The complete minor chord family in the key of C is displayed in Figure 6.

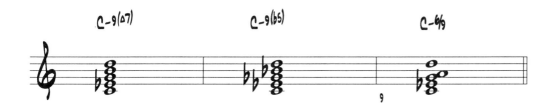

Figure 6. C Minor Chord Family

4.3 Dominant Chord Family

Dominant chords can be extended by adding thirds to the dominant seventh chord, yielding the extended dominant 9, 11, and 13 chords. Dominant chords can also be altered by adding a ♭5, ♯5, ♭9, or ♯9 to an extended chord (♭5 is synonymous with ♯11). With extensions and alterations, we have the mix of dominant chords in figure 7.

Figure 7. C Dominant Chord Family

4.4 Chord Outlining

Many of the chords described in the prior sections contain too many chord tones to be feasibly played on a standard six string guitar. In fact, many of the tones are superfluous to the overall sound of the chord. For example, dropping the 11th from a C13 chord results in very little overall change to the sound. To effectively play the chords we've described, we need to "compress" the chord using a form of lossy compression by dropping chord tones.

Chord quality is predominantly defined by the 3rd and 7th scale steps of a chord. When describing an extended chord (adding a 9th, 11th, or 13th) we require representation in the chord for the extension. Likewise, if a chord is altered (♭5, ♯5, ♭9, or ♯9) we require adequate representation of the respective alteration. Thus, it is feasible to outline most chords with just four tones.

Tables 1, 2, and 3 display the four chord tones which outline each chord described thus far. The remainder of the book demonstrates how to systematically map each four tone chord to the fretboard in multiple positions.

Table 1. Major Chord Family

	Chord	Symbol	Tones
1	Maj 7	Δ7	R 3 5 7
2	Maj 6	Δ6	R 3 5 6
3	Maj 7 b5	Δ7(b5), Δ7(#11)	R 3 b5 7
4	Maj Add 9	ΔAdd9	2 3 5 R
5	Maj 7w/9	Δ9	2 3 5 7
6	Maj 6/9	Δ6/9	2 3 5 6
7	Maj 7#5	Δ7(#5)	R 3 #5 7

Table 2. Minor Chord Family

	Chord	Symbol	Tones
1	Min 7	-7	R b3 5 b7
2	Min 6	-6	R b3 5 6
3	Min 7b5	-7(b5), ø	R b3 b5 b7
4	Min Add 9	-Add9	2 b3 5 R
5	Min 7 w/9	-9	2 b3 5 b7
6	Min / Maj 7	-(Δ7)	R b3 5 7
7	Min / Maj 7 w/9	-9(Δ7)	2 b3 5 7
8	Min 7b5 w/9	-9(b5)	2 b3 b5 b7
9	Min 6 w/9	-6/9	2 b3 5 6

Table 5. Dominant Chord Family

	Chord	Symbol	Tones
1	Dom 7	7	R 3 5 b7
2	Dom 7b5	7(b5), 7(#11)	R 3 b5 b7
3	Dom 7 #5	7(#5), +7, aug7	R 3 #5 b7
4	Dom 9	9	2 3 5 b7
5	Dom 9 b5	9(b5), 9(#11)	2 3 b5 b7
6	Dom 9 #5	9(#5)	2 3 #5 b7
7	Dom 13	13	R 3 6 b7
8	Dom 13 w/9	13 add9	2 3 6 b7
9	Dom 7b9	7(b9)	b2 3 5 b7
10	Dom 7 #9	7(#9)	#2 3 5 b7
11	Dom 7 #5b9	C7(b9/#5), +7(b9)	b2 3 #5 b7
12	Dom 7 #5#9	7(#9/#5), +7(#9)	#2 3 #5 b7
13	Dom 13 b9	13(b9)	b2 3 6 b7
14	Dom 13 #9	13(#9)	#2 3 6 b7
15	Dom 7b5b9	7(b9/b5)	b2 3 b5 b7
16	Dom 7b5#9	7(#9/b5)	#2 3 b5 b7
17	Dom 7 sus	7sus, 11	R 4 5 b7

All chords displayed in this book are movable, and can be played in all twelve keys by sliding the chord position up or down the fretboard. Chords are displayed in the key of C, and other keys can be determined from the Chord Transposition Matrix displayed in table 4.

Table 4. Chord Transposition Matrix

0	C	Db	D	Eb	E	F	Gb	G	Ab	A	Bb	B
1	Db	D	Eb	E	F	Gb	G	Ab	A	Bb	B	C
2	D	Eb	E	F	Gb	G	Ab	A	Bb	B	C	Db
3	Eb	E	F	Gb	G	Ab	A	Bb	B	C	Db	D
4	E	F	Gb	G	Ab	A	Bb	B	C	Db	D	Eb
5	F	Gb	G	Ab	A	Bb	B	C	Db	D	Eb	E
6	Gb	G	Ab	A	Bb	B	C	Db	D	Eb	E	F
7	G	Ab	A	Bb	B	C	Db	D	Eb	E	F	Gb
8	Ab	A	Bb	B	C	Db	D	Eb	E	F	Gb	G
9	A	Bb	B	C	Db	D	Eb	E	F	Gb	G	Ab
10	Bb	B	C	Db	D	Eb	E	F	Gb	G	Ab	A
11	B	C	Db	D	Eb	E	F	Gb	G	Ab	A	Bb

For example, if a chord is in the key of G on the sixth fret, and the playing situation requires the same chord in the key of D, determine the chord position as follows:

Scan down the first column until you see the number 6 (indicating your current position), then move to the right until you see the letter G. Next move up the G column until you reach the letter D (indicating your desired key). The number in the first column indicates the fret required to play the desired chord in D, which is fret 1. Adjust for enharmonics if a key uses sharps, e.g. Gb equals F#. Eventually you need to perform key transposition on-the-fly.

Table 5 on page 16 displays the number of chords at your disposal using the chord system. There are a finite number of chords and physical positions playable on the fretboard on a per series basis. Multiplying the number of chords by playable positions in each series and adding the individual subtotals yields a total of 17,784 chords at your disposal.

Table 5. Chord Palette

Series	Chords	Positions	Keys	Subtotal
Low Density	33	12	12	4,752
Medium Density	33	8	12	3,168
High Density	33	8	12	3,168
Cluster	33	10	12	3,960
Ninth	19	12	12	2,736
			Total	17,784

Root position chord inversion involves taking a chord in root position, and raising notes an octave within the chord. Figure 8 displays the root position $C^{\Delta7}$ chord, and it's three inversions.

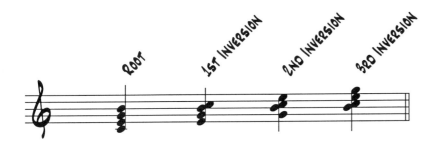

Figure 8. $C^{\Delta7}$ Root position chord inversion

The root position $C^{\Delta7}$ chord is built from root, major third, perfect fifth, and major seventh. The first inversion raises the root an octave, the second inversion raises the third an octave, and finally – the third inversion raises the fifth an octave.

Figure 9 displays root position chord inversions with numeric scale positions for each chord tone.

Figure 9. $C^{\Delta7}$ root position chord inversion with scale positions

Root position $C^{\Delta7}$ provides one chord series, and many other potential series exist. Yet only a handful are practical for playing a six-string guitar with standard tuning. The first series is the "Low Density Series" displayed in Figure 10.

In this book, we limit ourselves to the five chord series displayed in figure 11.

The first three series vary "density" by increasing the distance between bottom and top notes as you progress from low, to medium, then high densities. The cluster series is the standard root $^{\Delta7}$ chord formation discussed earlier, and the ninth series is applicable to chords containing a 9, #9, or ♭9.

Figure 10. Low Density Series C△7

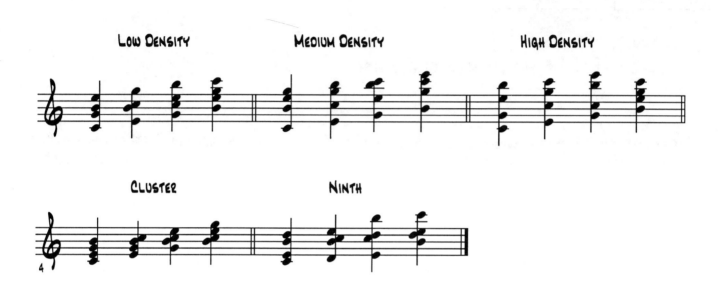

Figure 11. Inversion Series

For review, the low density C∆7 series is:

Figure 12. Low Density Series C∆7

We now map the four note chords displayed in Table 1, Table 2, and Table 3 starting on page 13 onto the Low Density Series in Figure 12. Figure 13 displays the low density C-7 voicing, and Figure 14 displays the low density C7 voicing.

Figure 13. Low Density Series C-7

Figure 14. Low Density Series C7

Each of the four note chords in Figure 12 can be played using each of the above voicings on three vertical areas of the neck:

1. lowest note on the sixth string (Bottom Set)

2. lowest note on the fifth string (Middle Set)

3. lowest note on the fourth string (Top Set)

This results in 12 total chords (4 voicings per vertical area) per chord configuration.

5.1.1 Major Chord Family

In the following pages, all chords in Table 1, Table 2, and Table 3 are mapped onto the three vertical areas of the neck in each of the four voicings. The pages are logically grouped, with the resulting 12 chords (four voicings per area).

Pay particular attention to the fingering and chord tones.

CΔ7

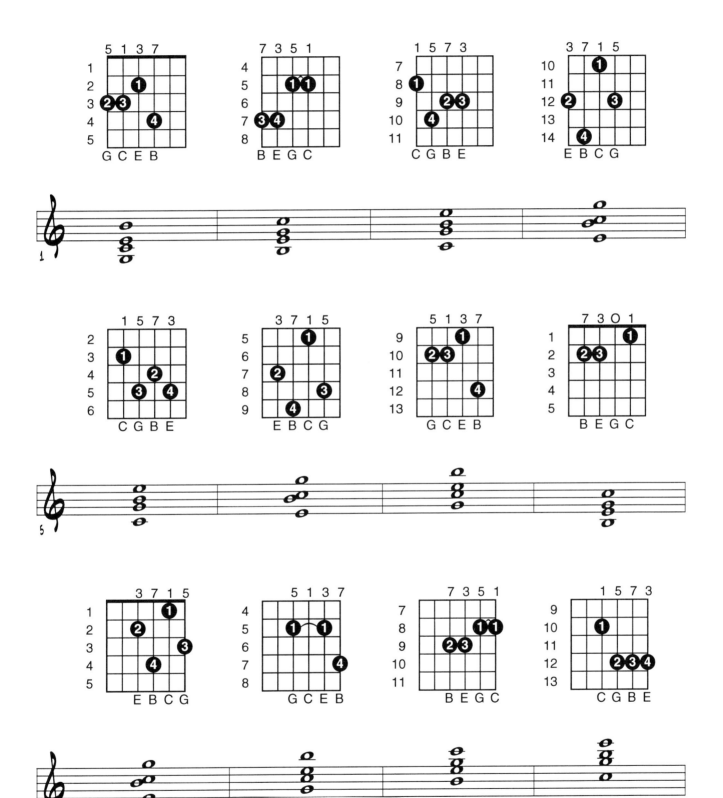

C△6

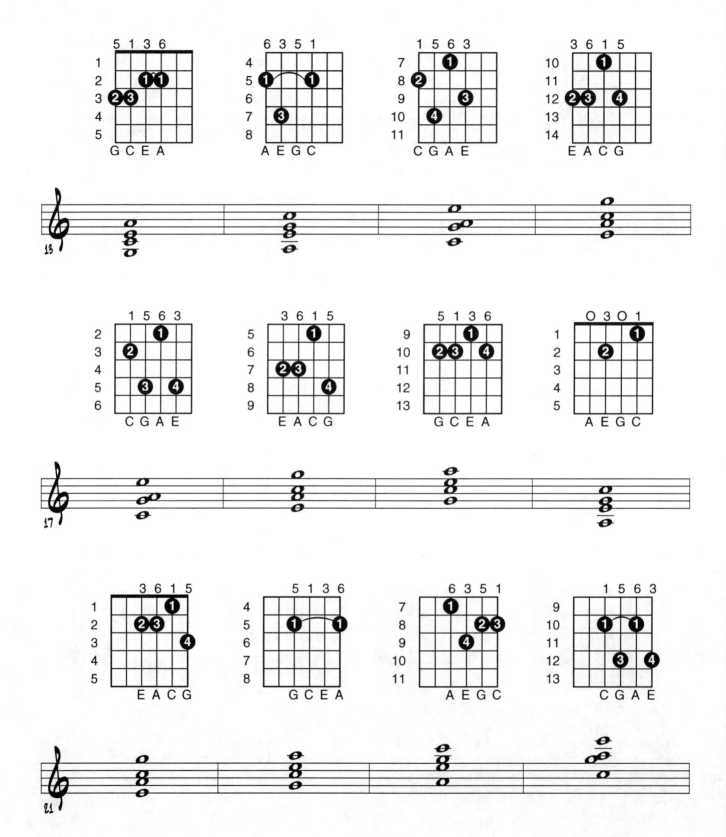

C△7(♭5)

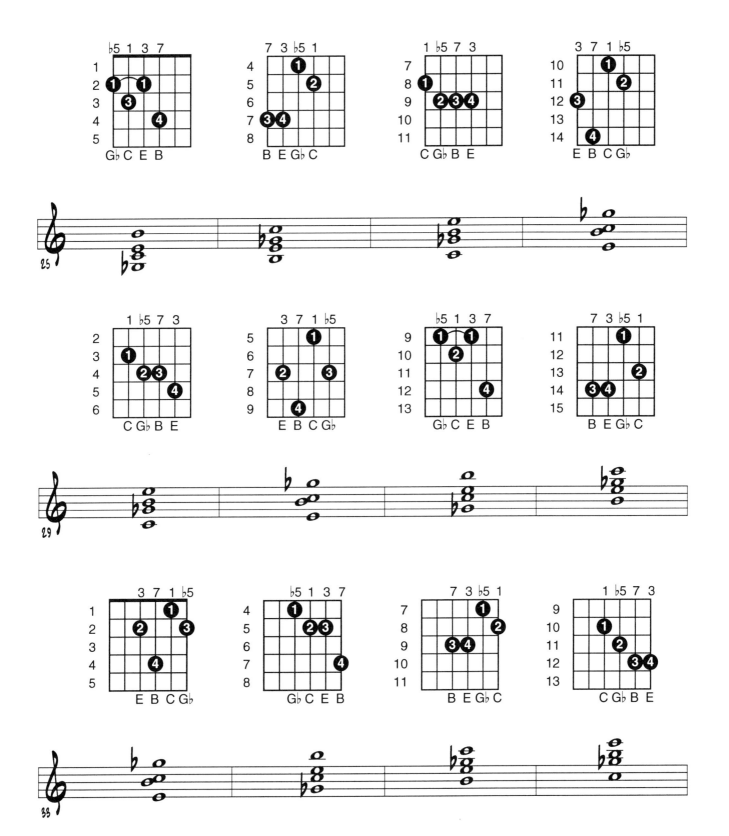

C△add9

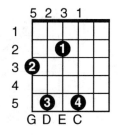
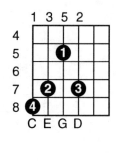
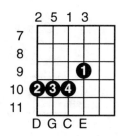
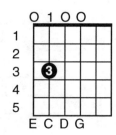

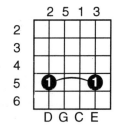
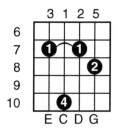
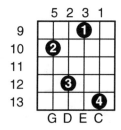
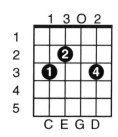

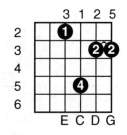
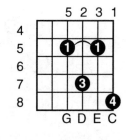
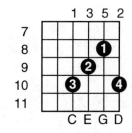
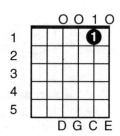

C△9

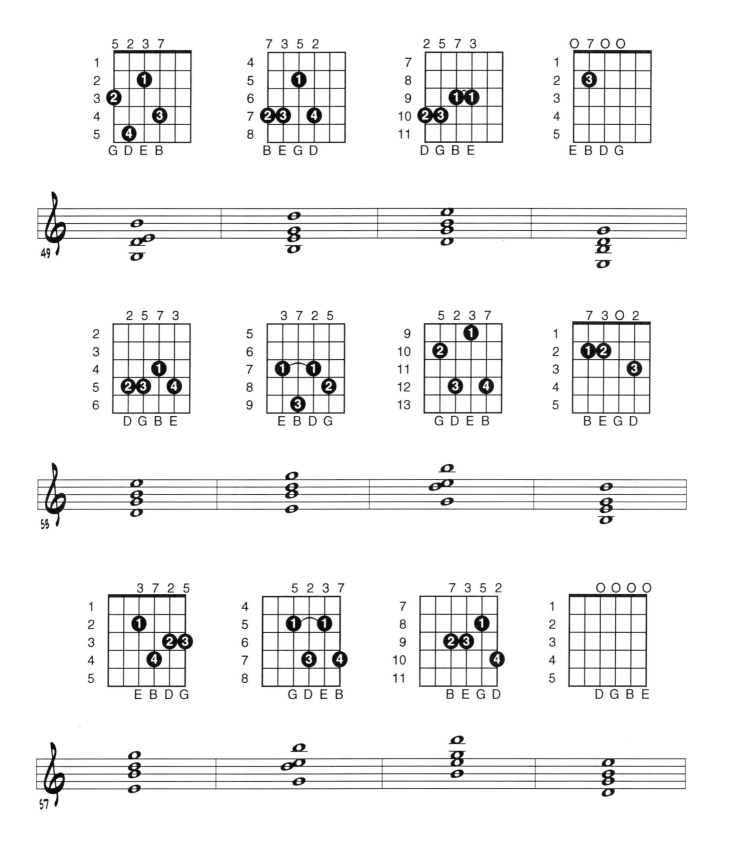

25

C△6/9

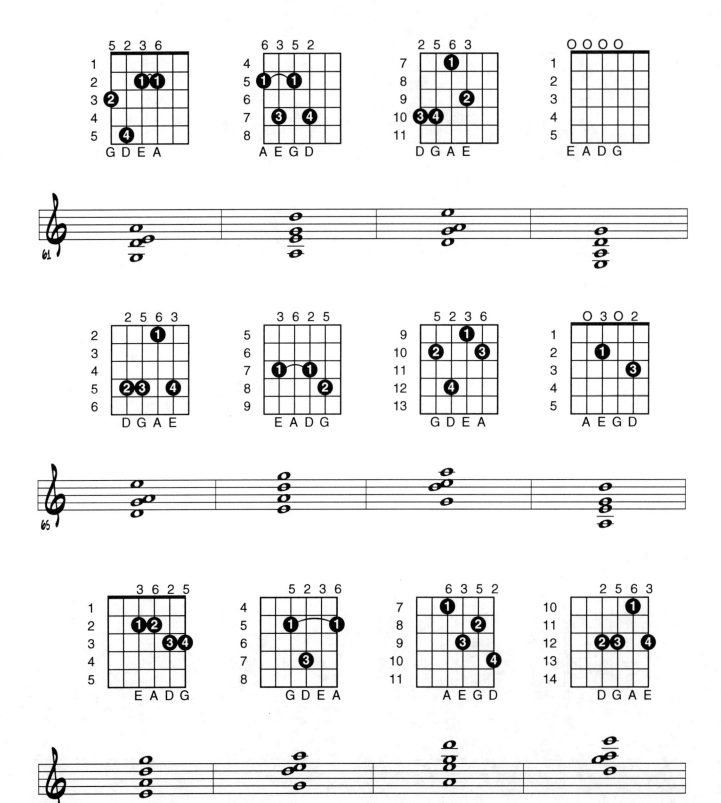

C△7(#5)

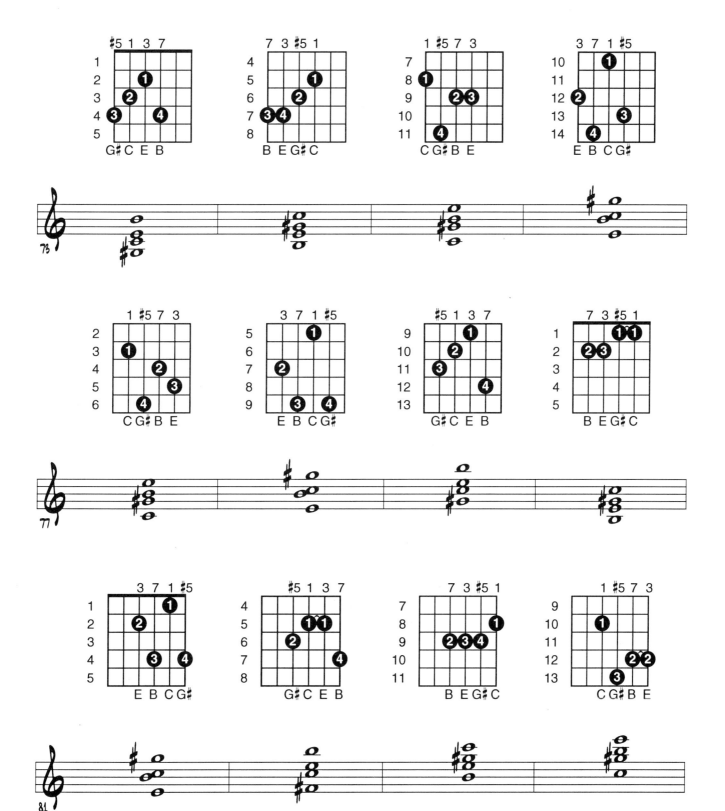

27

5.1.2 Minor Chord Family

C-7

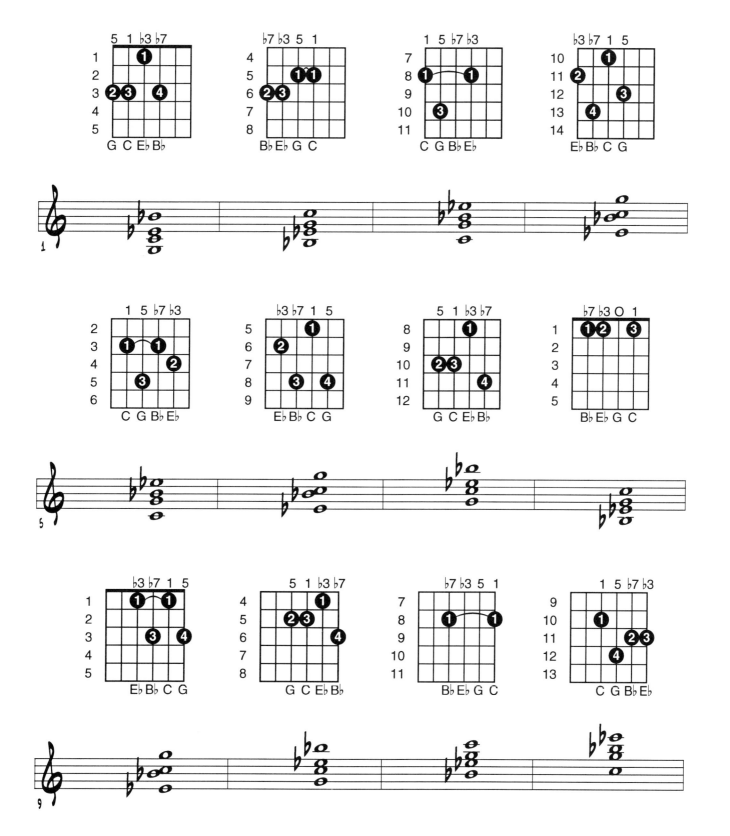

C-6

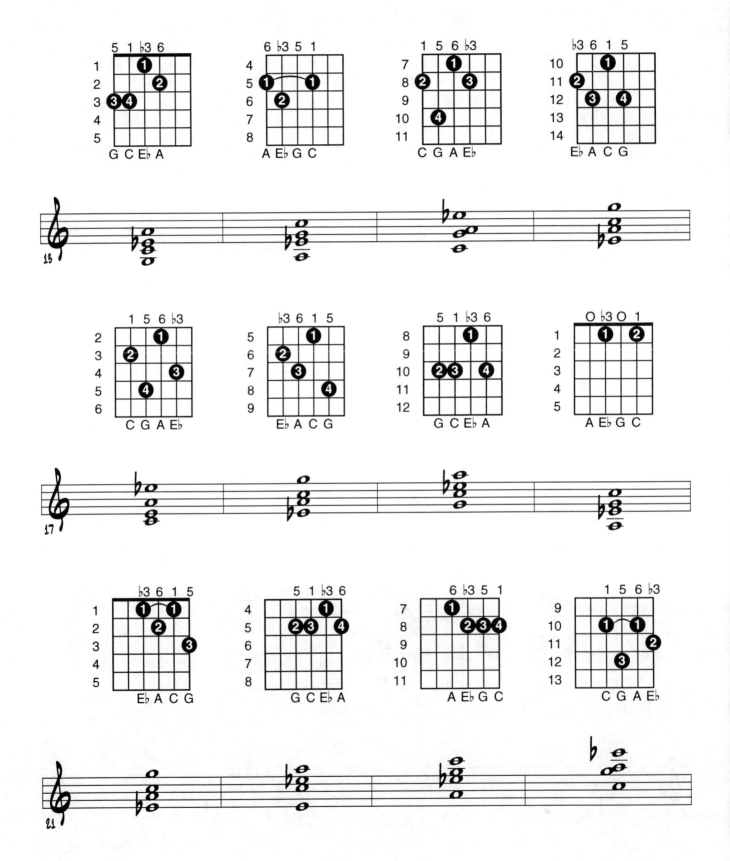

C-7(b5)

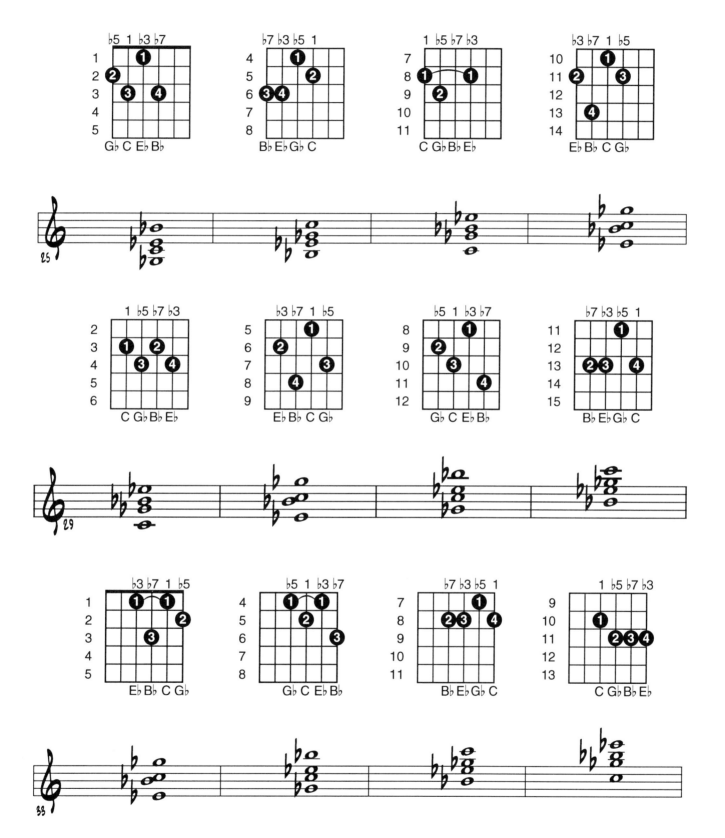

C-ADD9

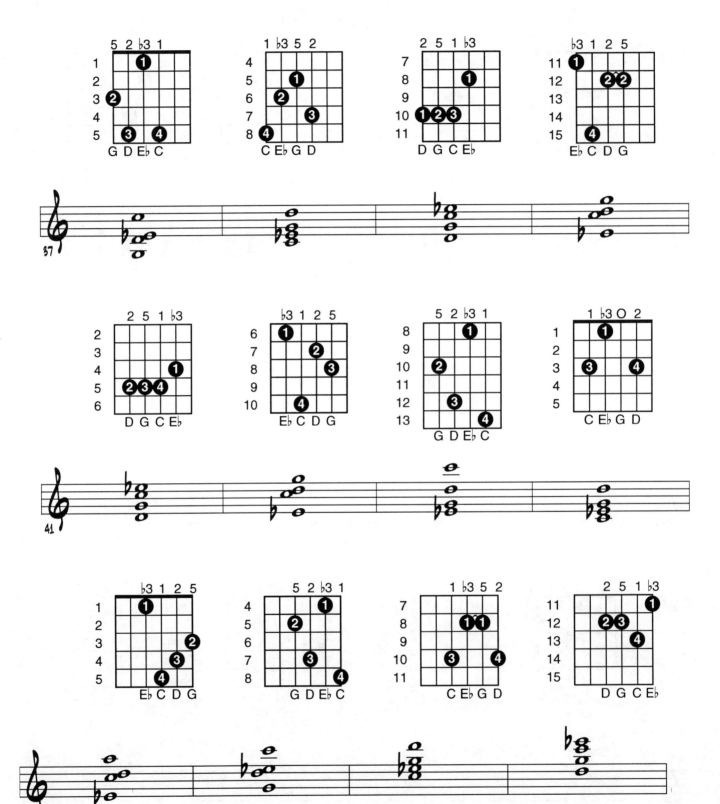

C-9

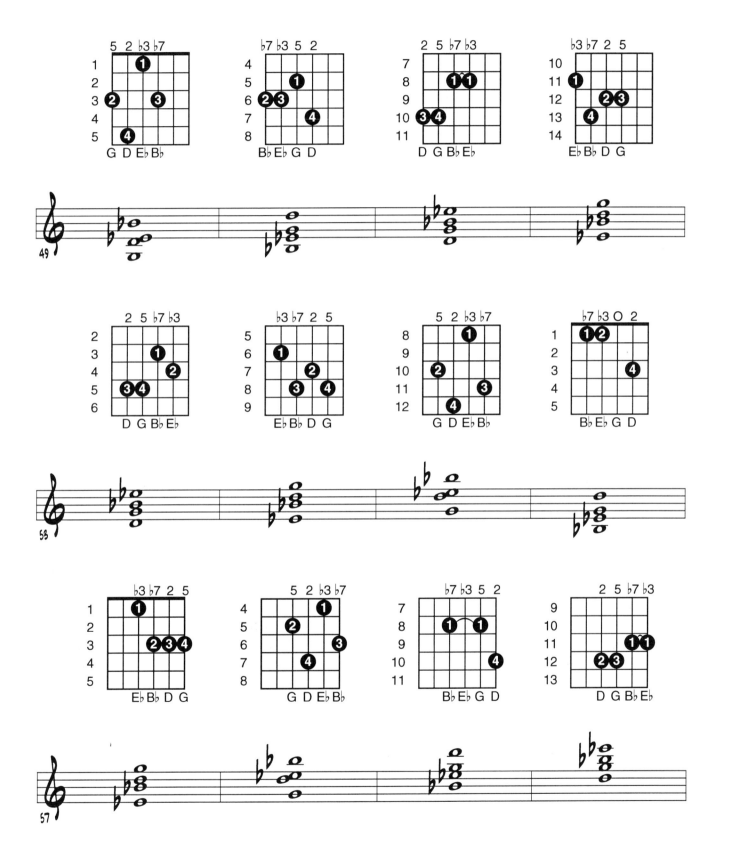

C-(Δ7)

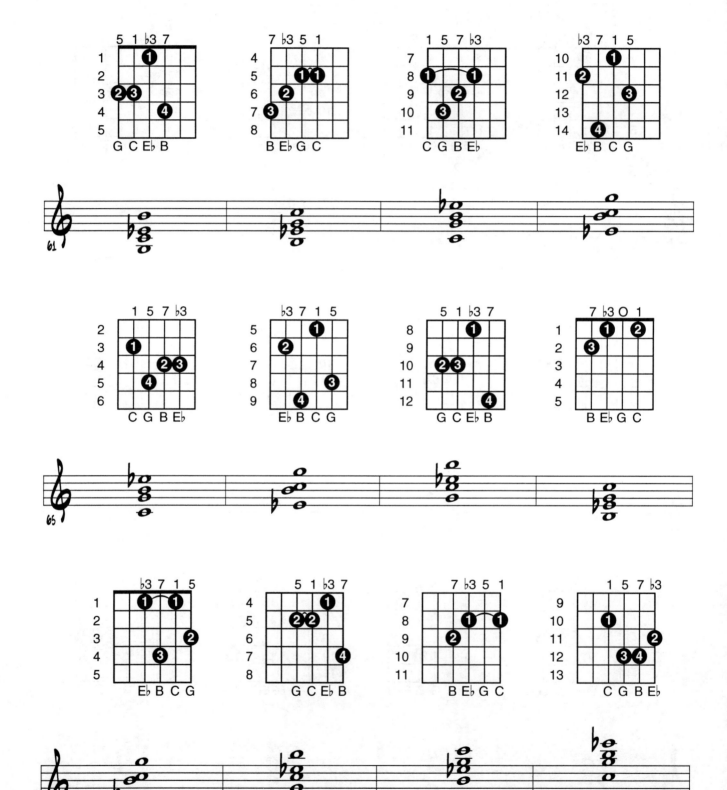

C-9(Δ7)

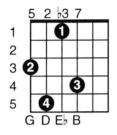
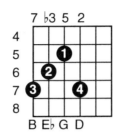
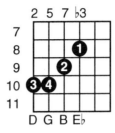
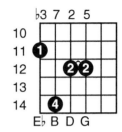

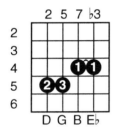
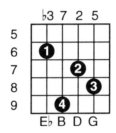
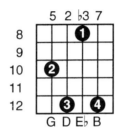
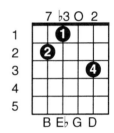

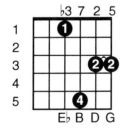
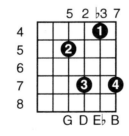
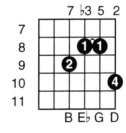
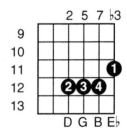

C-9(b5)

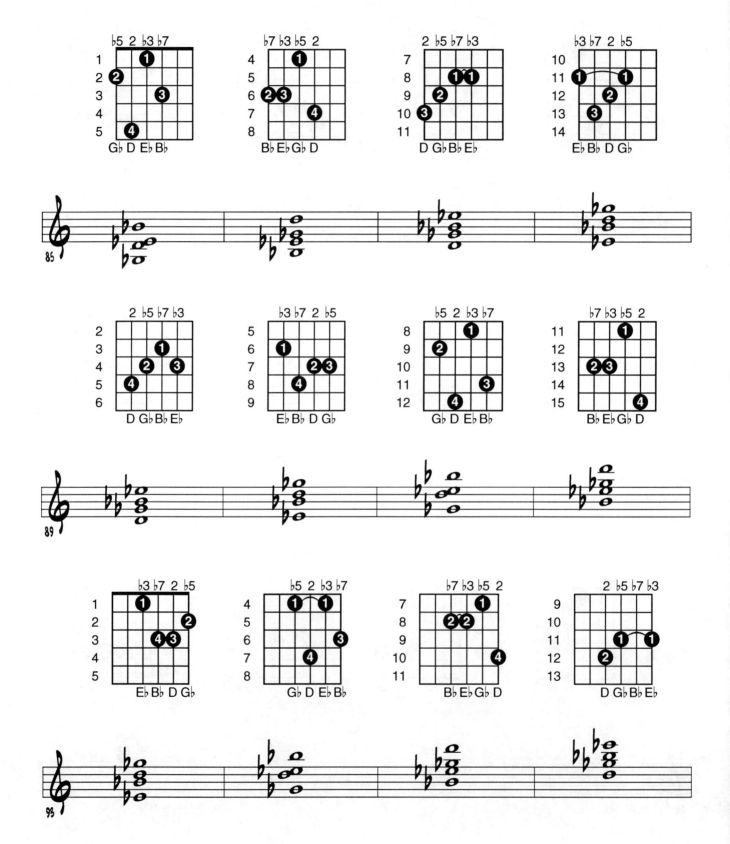

C-6/9

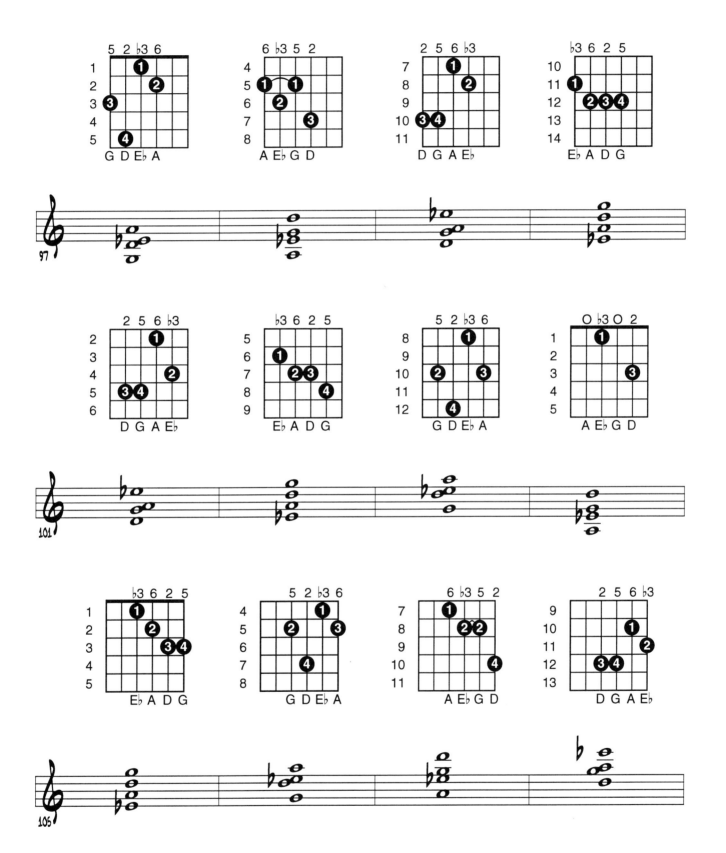

5.1.3 Dominant Chord Family

C7

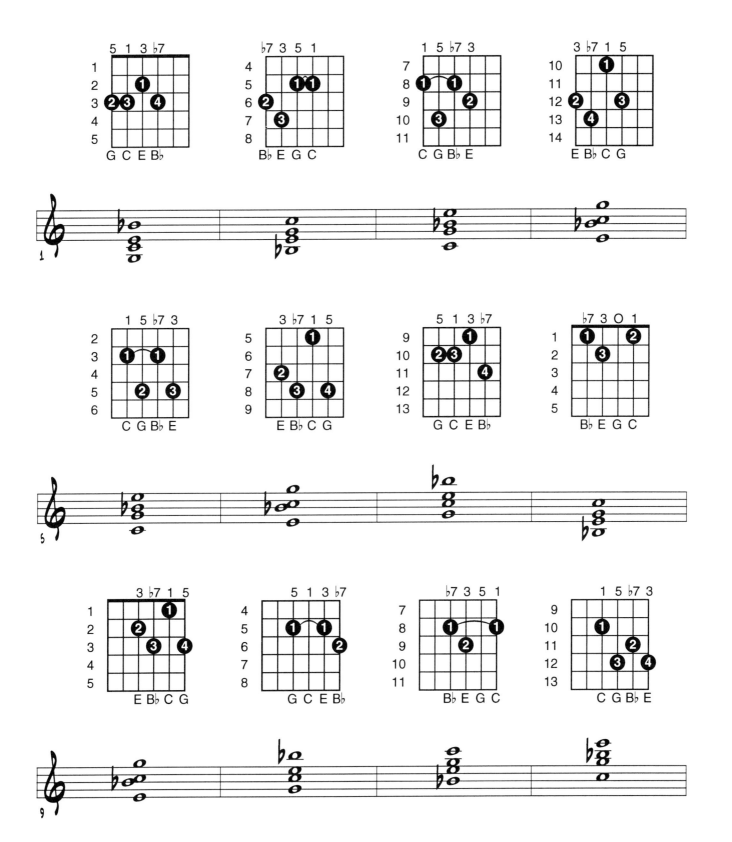

LOW DENSITY SERIES

C7(b5)

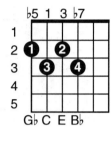

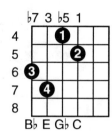

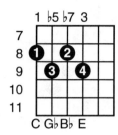

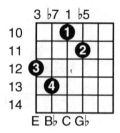

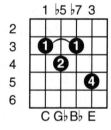

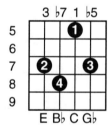

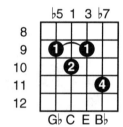

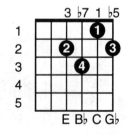

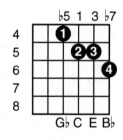

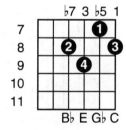

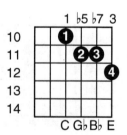

C7(#5)

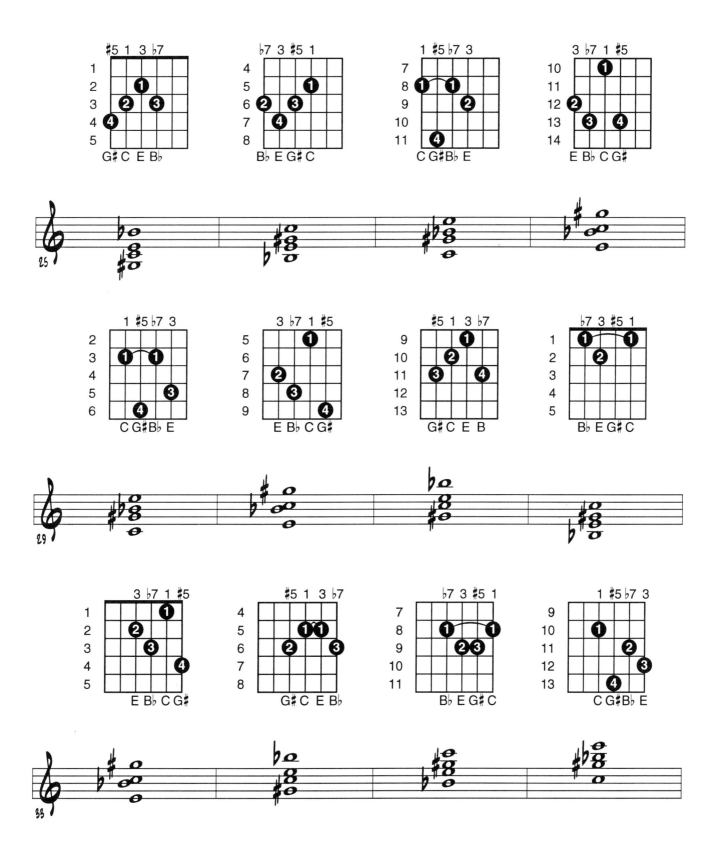

41

C9

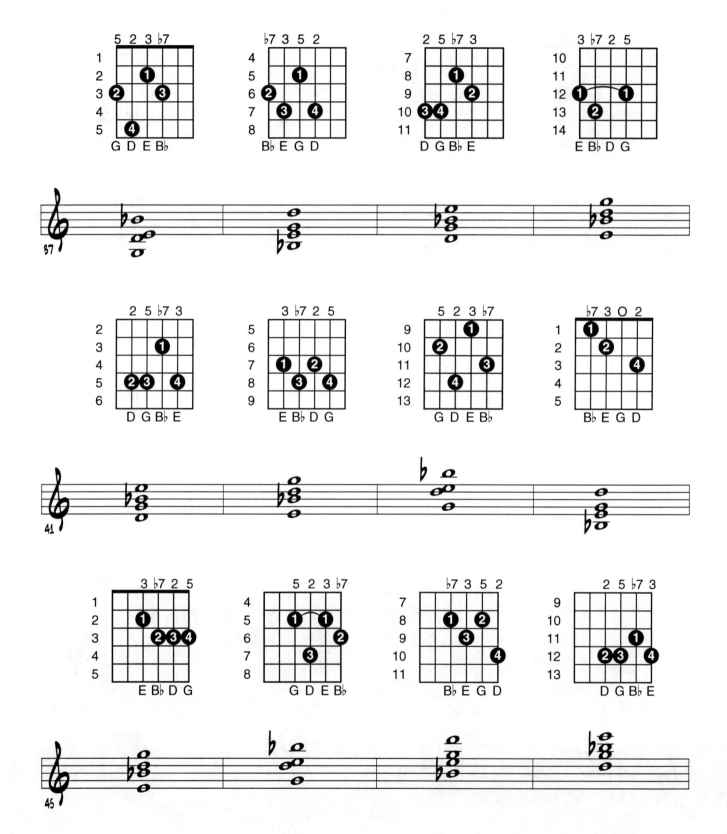

C9(b5)

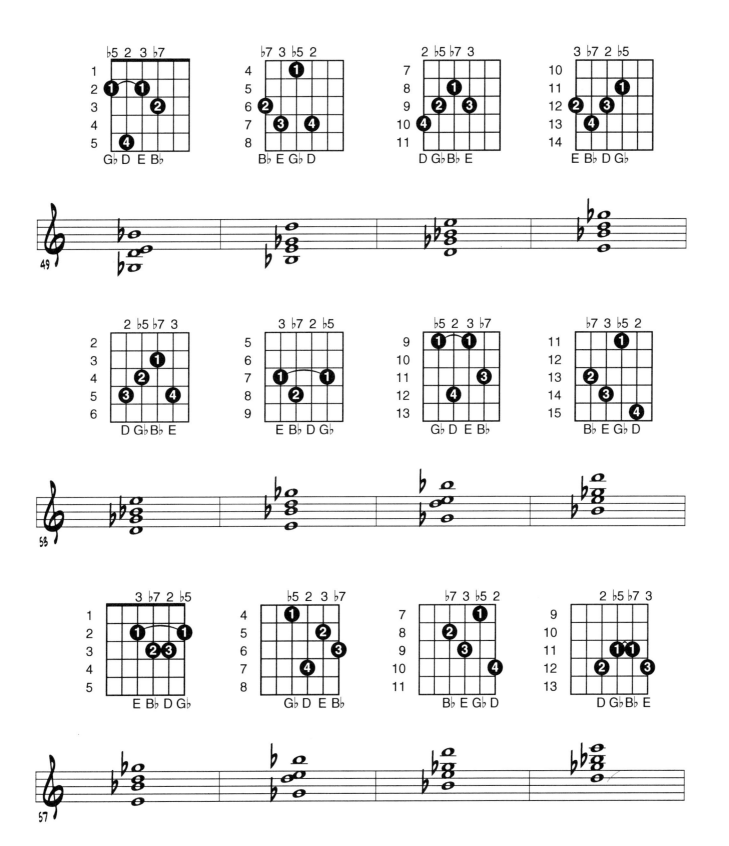

C9(#5)

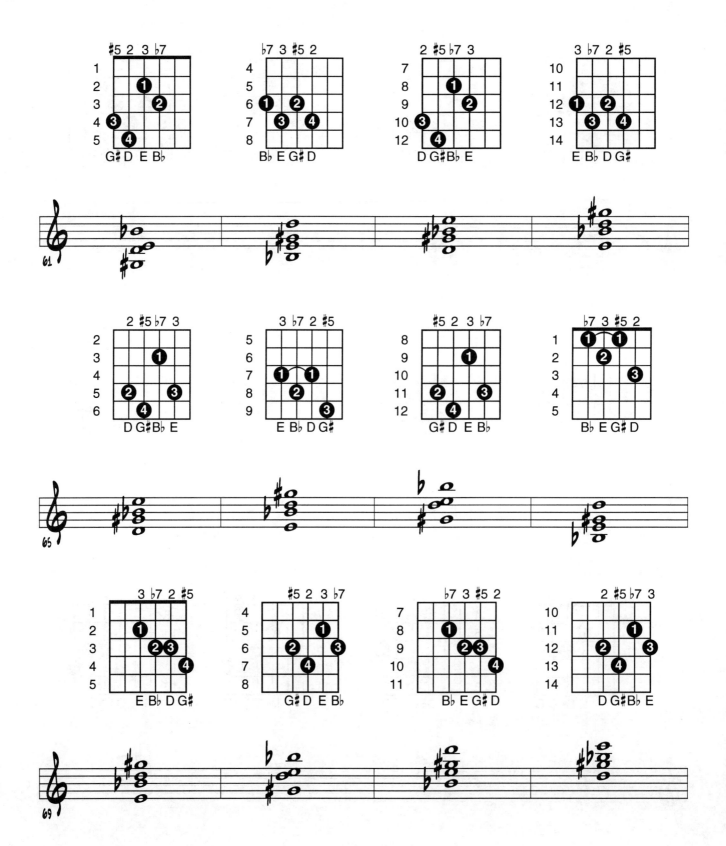

C13

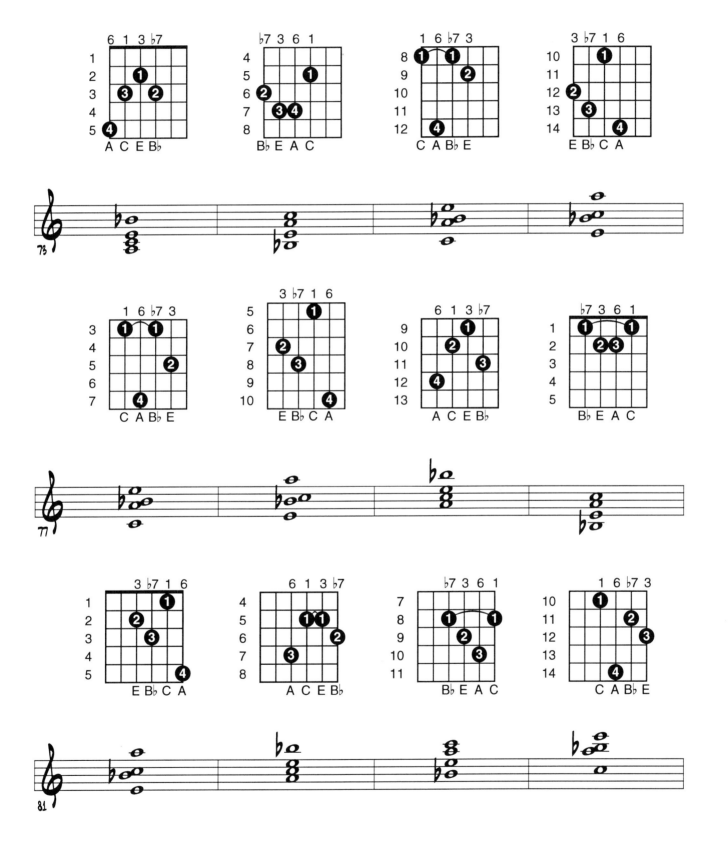

C13add9

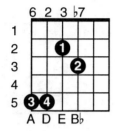
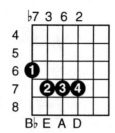
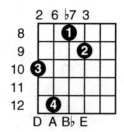

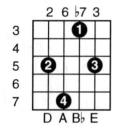
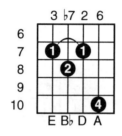
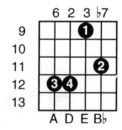
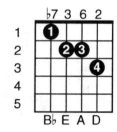

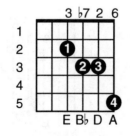
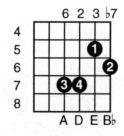
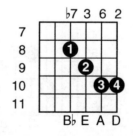
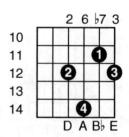

C7(b9)

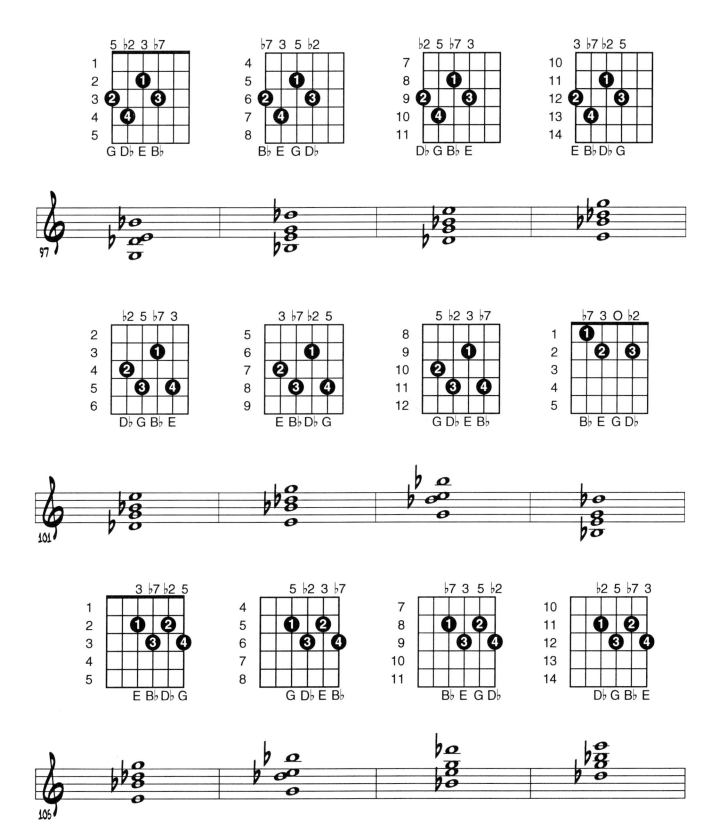

47

C7(#9)

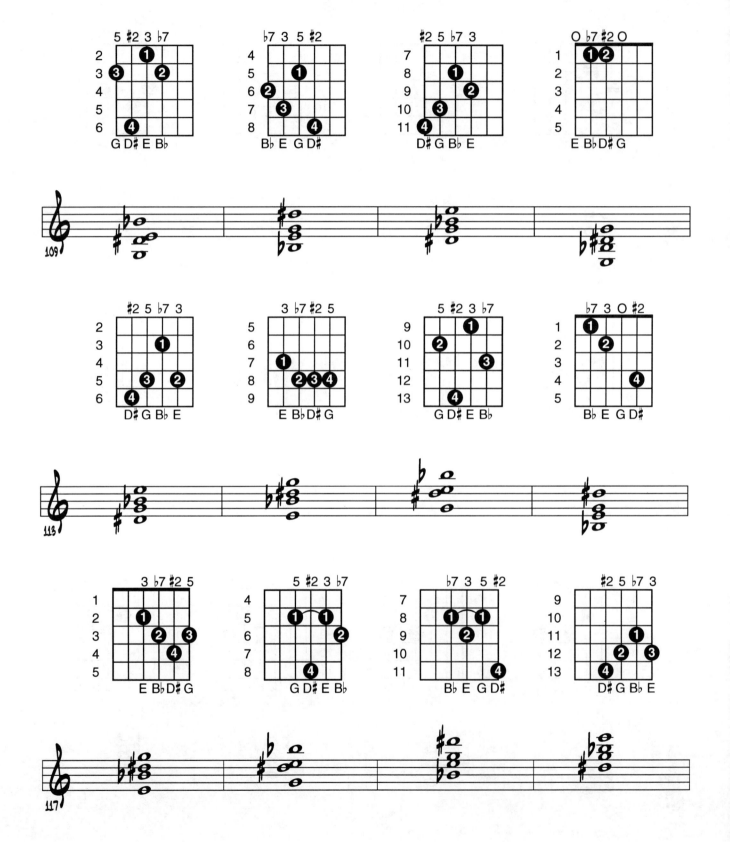

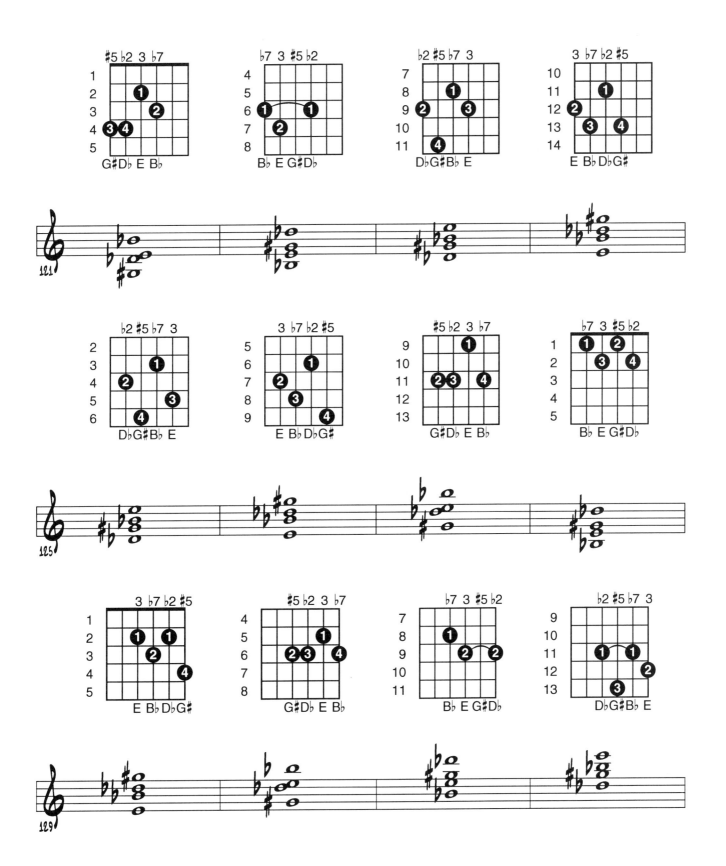

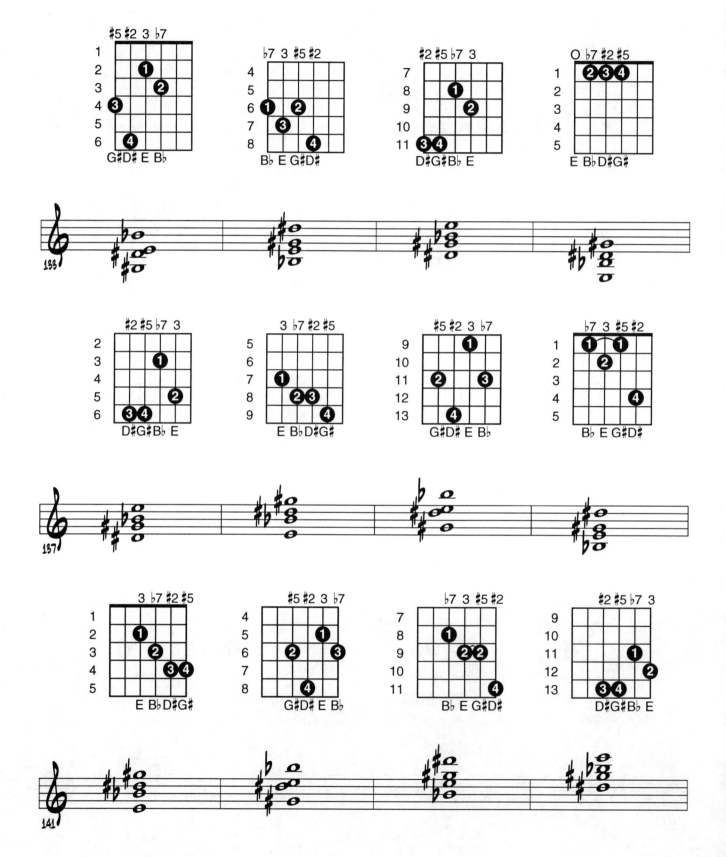

C13(b9)

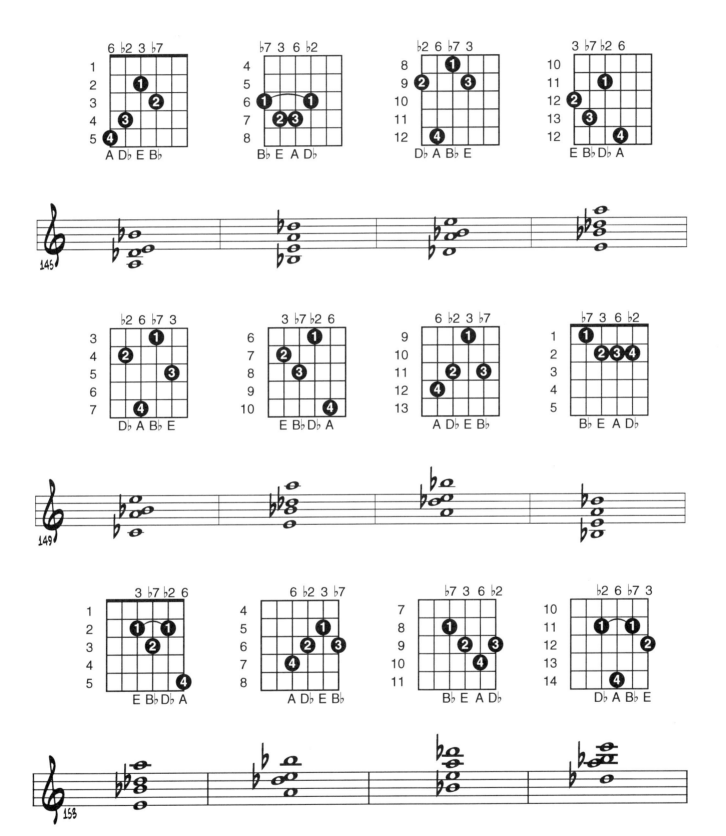

C13(♯9)

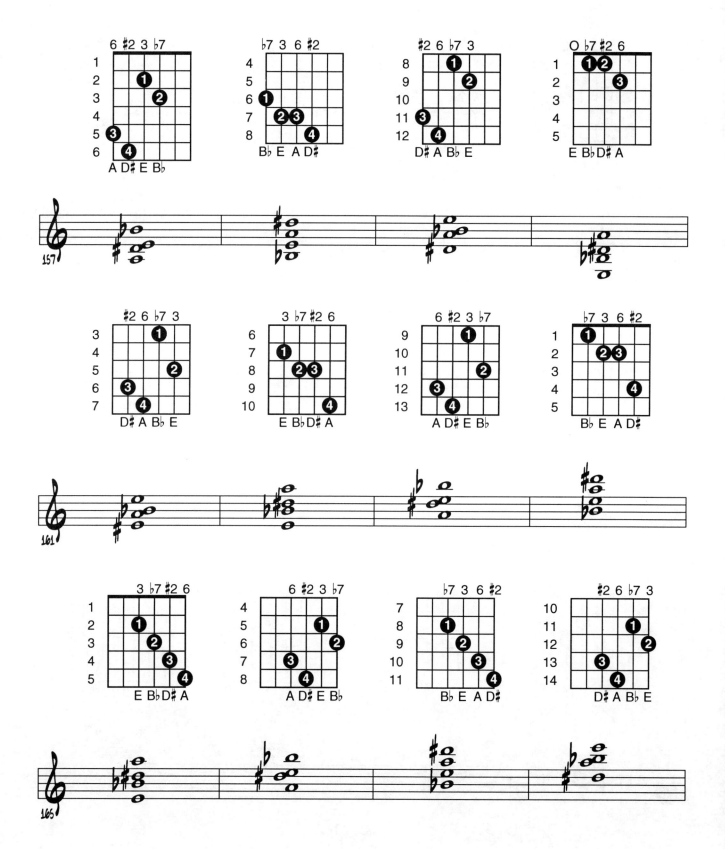

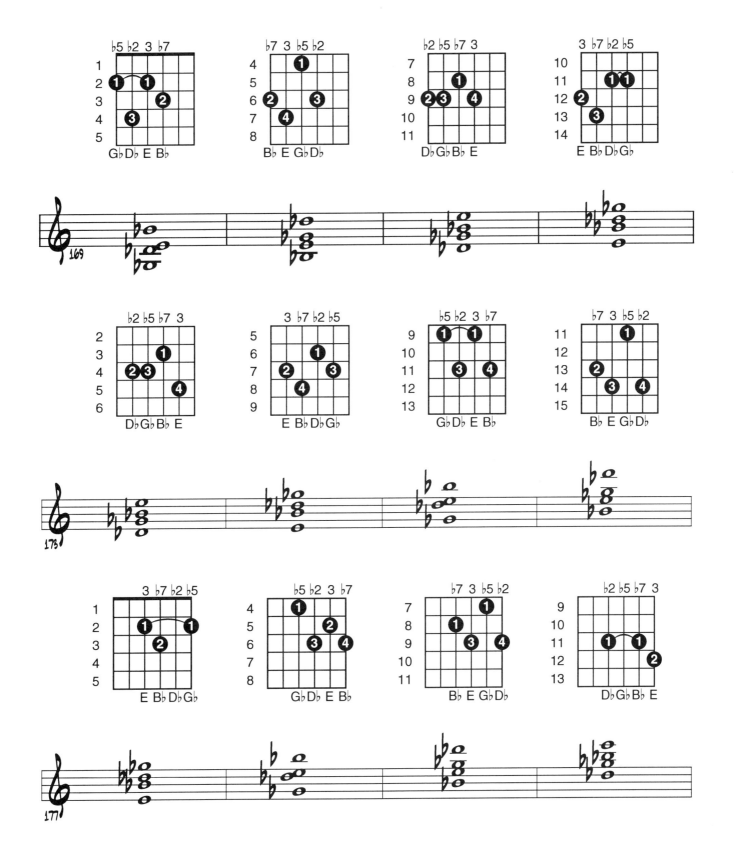

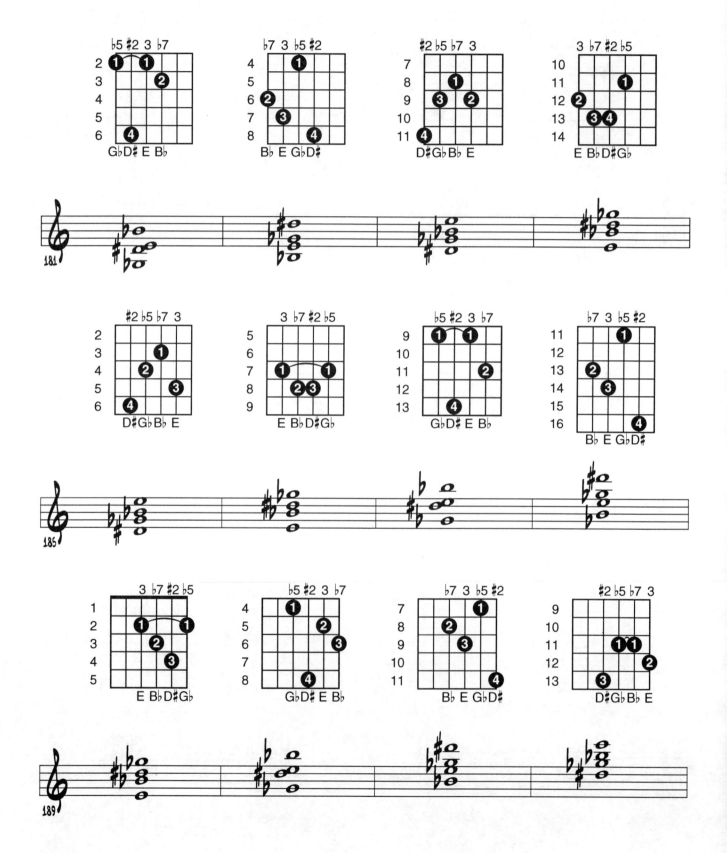

C7sus

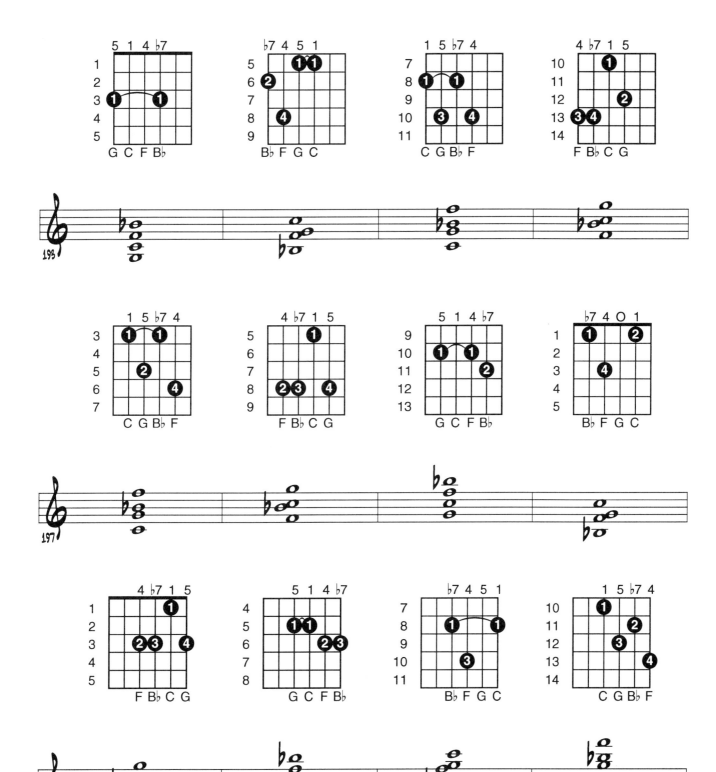

LOW DENSITY SERIES

5.3 Medium Density Series

The medium density series builds upon the low density series (figure 10 on page 18) by moving the second tone from the bottom up an octave.

Figure 15. Medium Density Series C△7

Each of the four note chords in Figure 15 can be played on two vertical areas of the neck:

1. Lowest note on the sixth string (Bottom Set)

2. Lowest note on the fifth string (Top Set)

This results in 8 total chords (4 voicings per veritical area) per chord configuration

5.3.1 Major Chord Family

On the following pages, all chords in table 1, table 2, and table 3 are mapped onto both vertical areas. The pages contain two voicings per page, with the resulting 8 chords (four voicings per area).

CΔ7

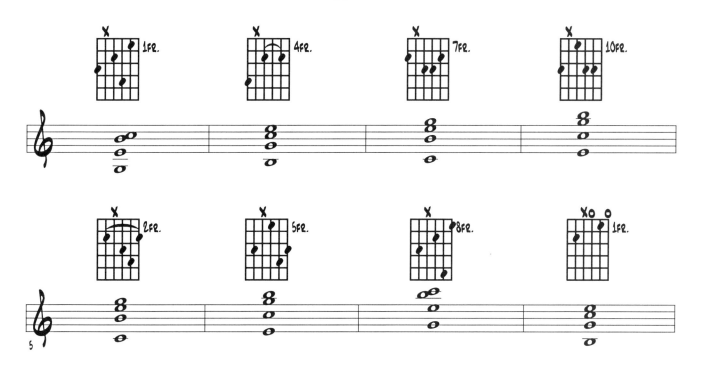

CΔ6

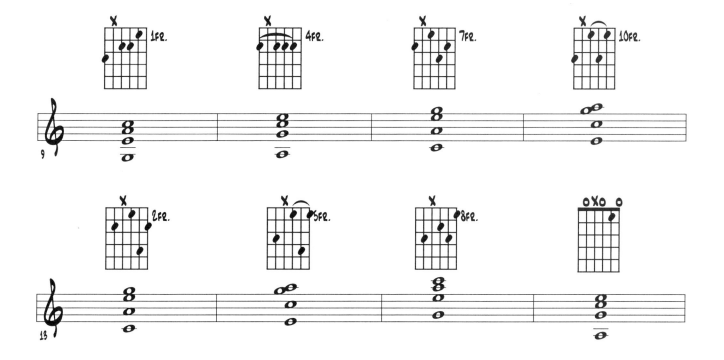

57

C△7(b5)

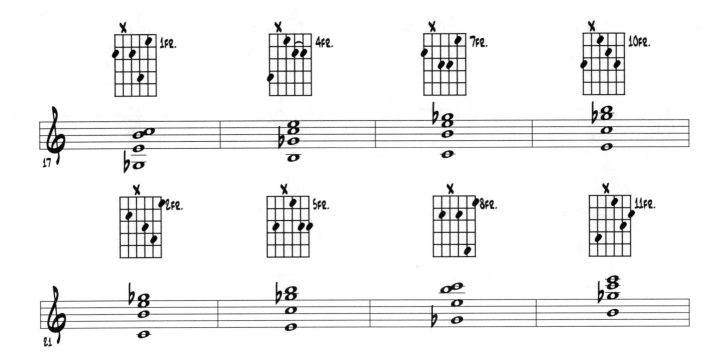

C△ADD9

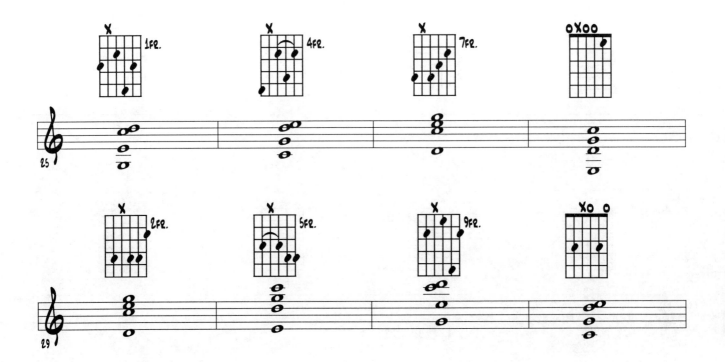

C△9

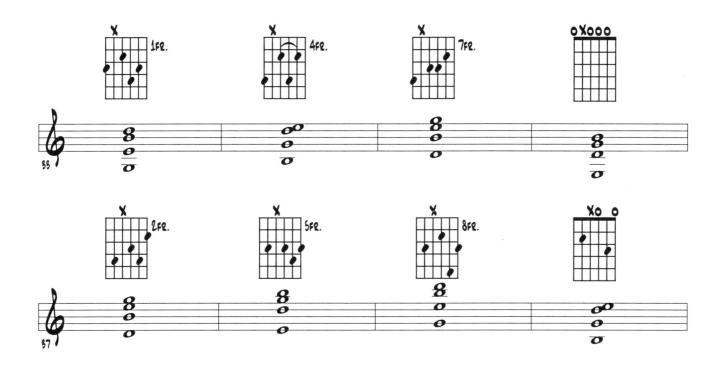

C△6/9

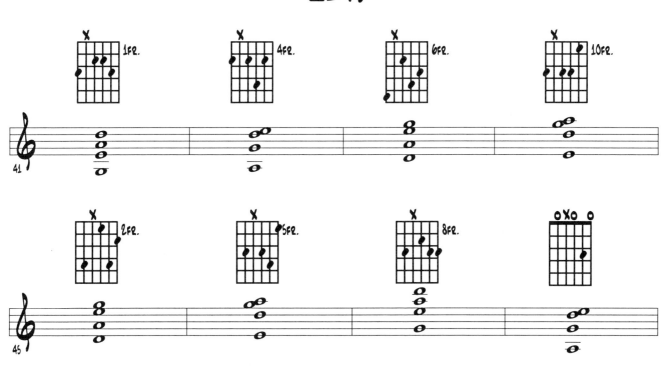

59

C△7(#5)

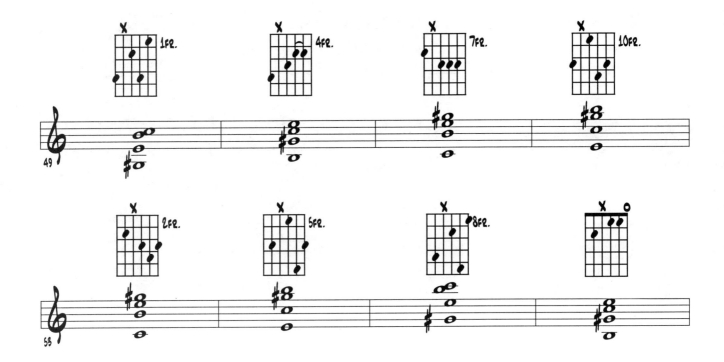

C-7

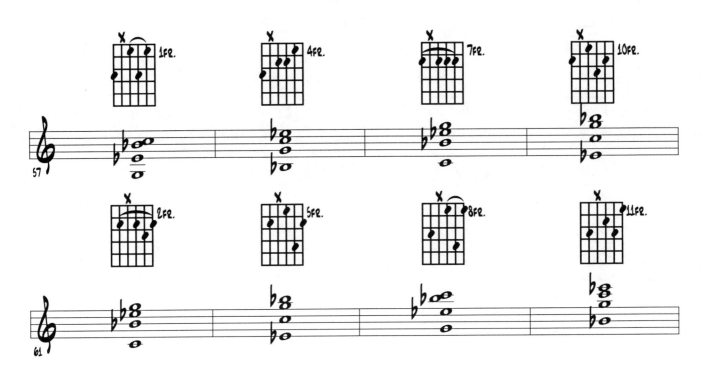

C-6

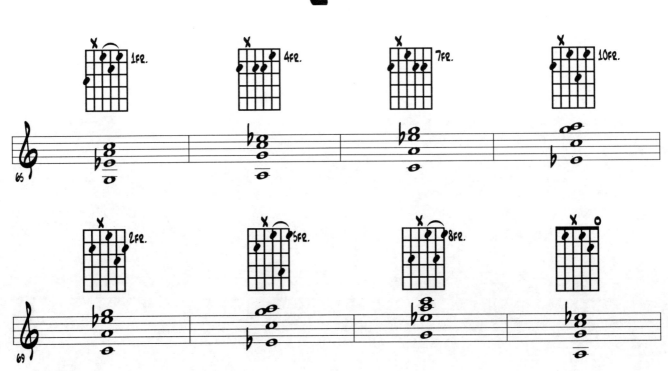

C-7(b5)

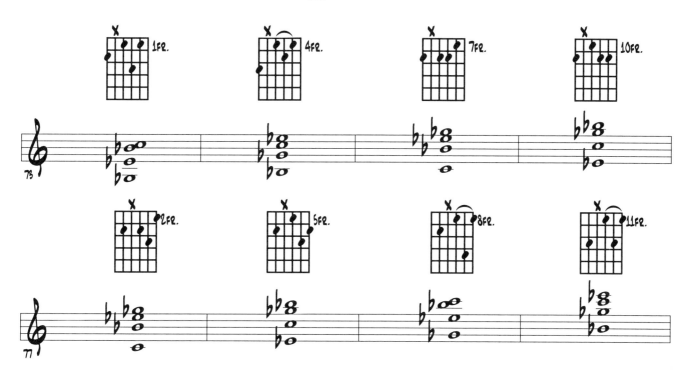

C-ADD9

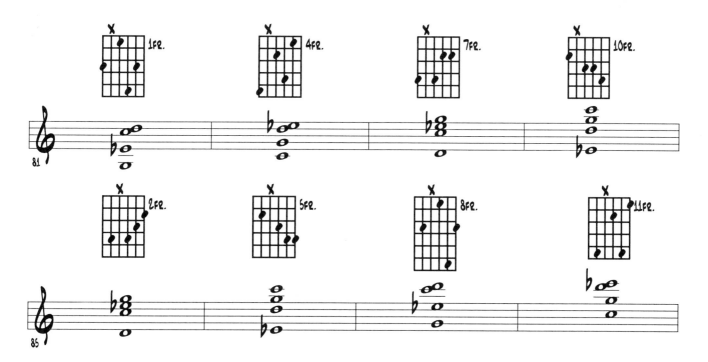

C-9

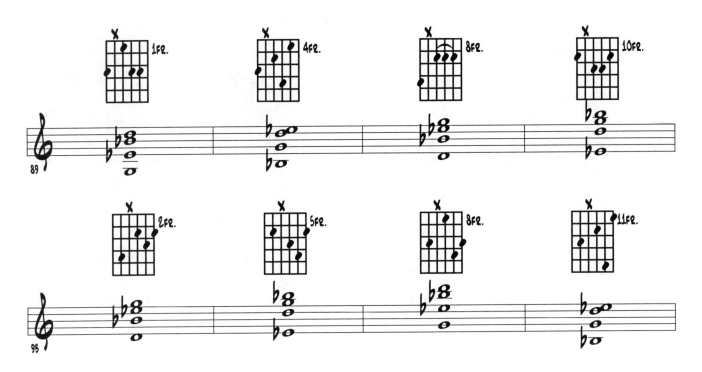

C-(Δ7)

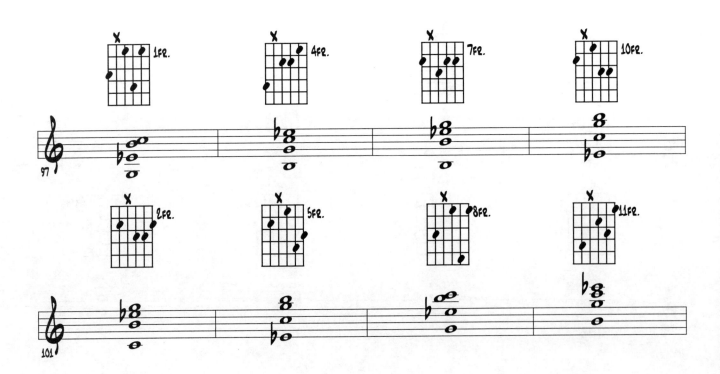

C-9(Δ7)

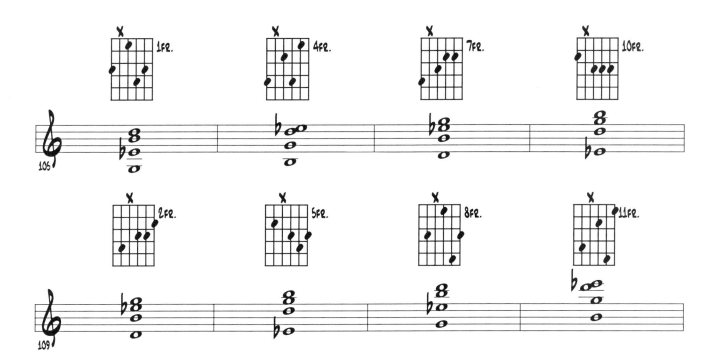

C-9(b5)

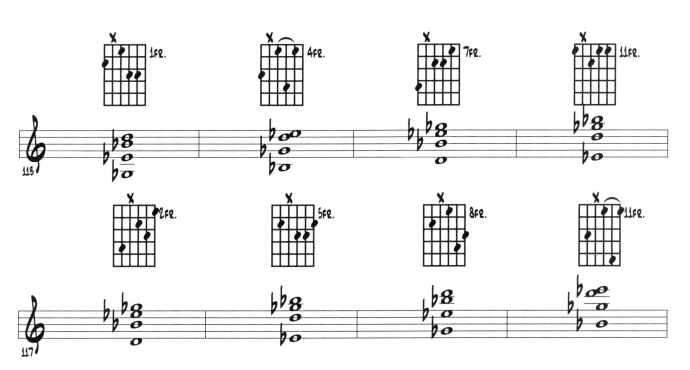

C-6/9

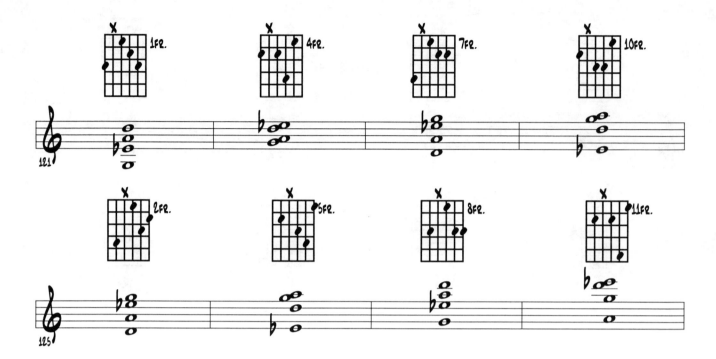

C7

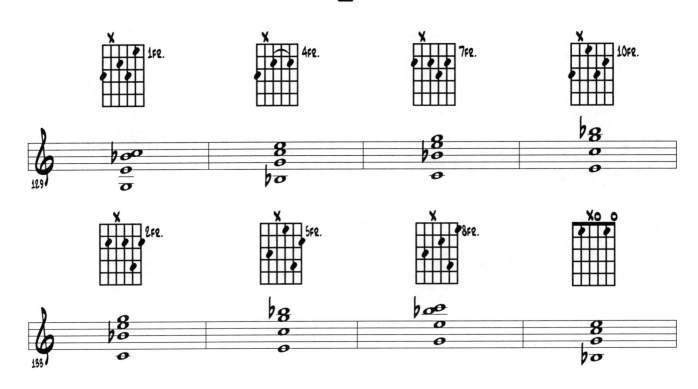

C7(b5)

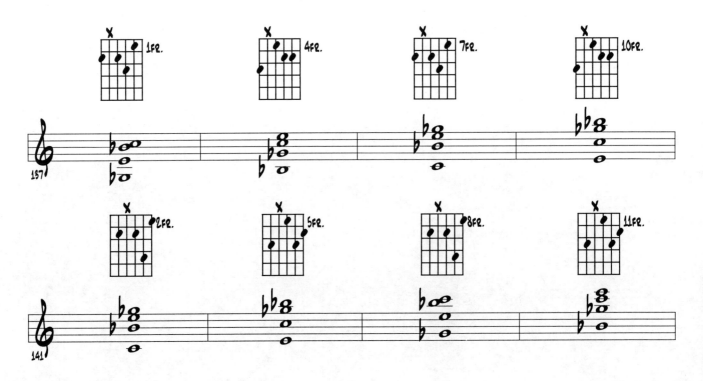

C7(♯5)

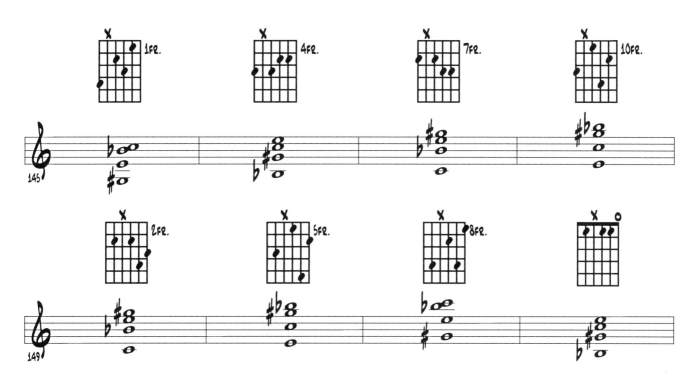

C9

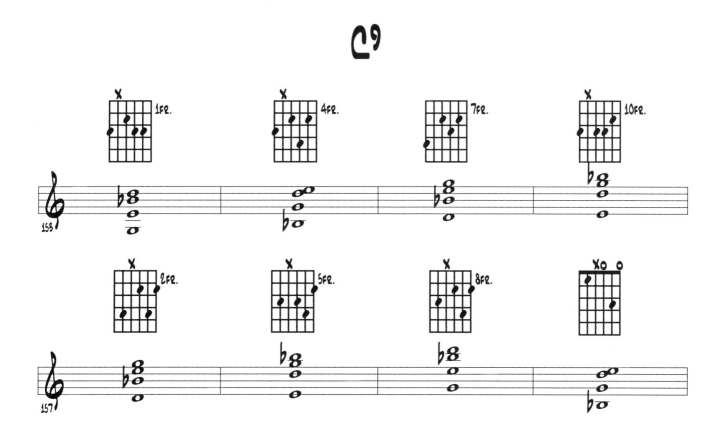

69

C9(b5)

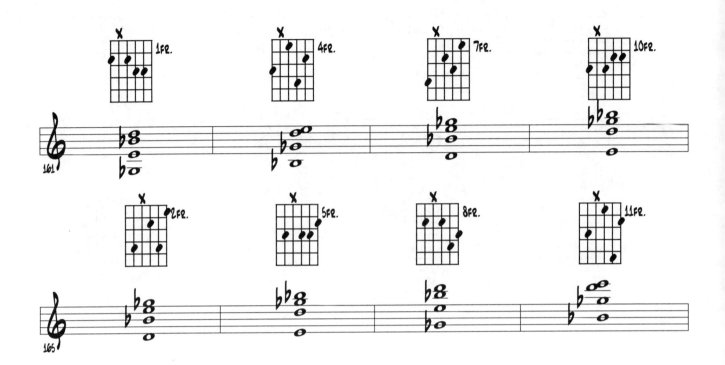

C9(#5)

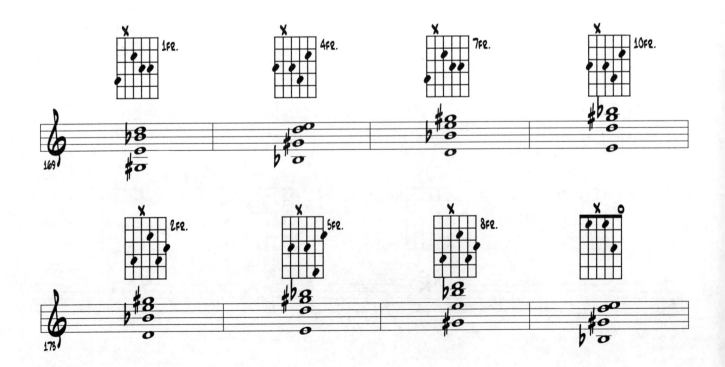

C13

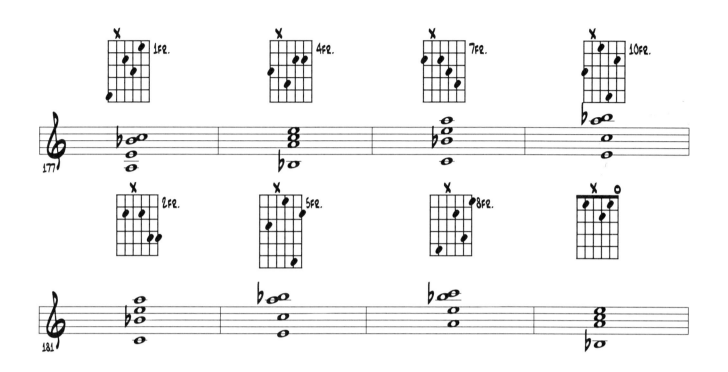

C13ADD9

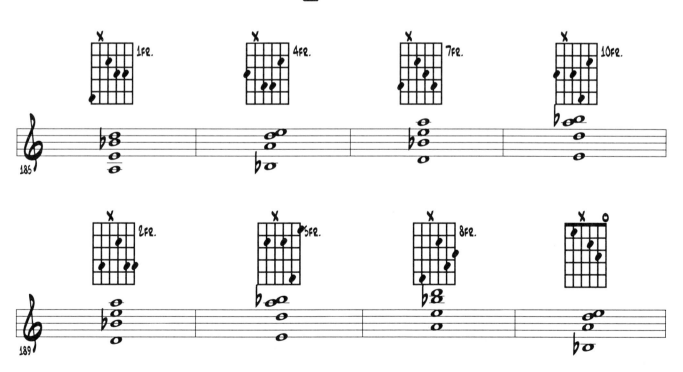

71

C7(♭9)

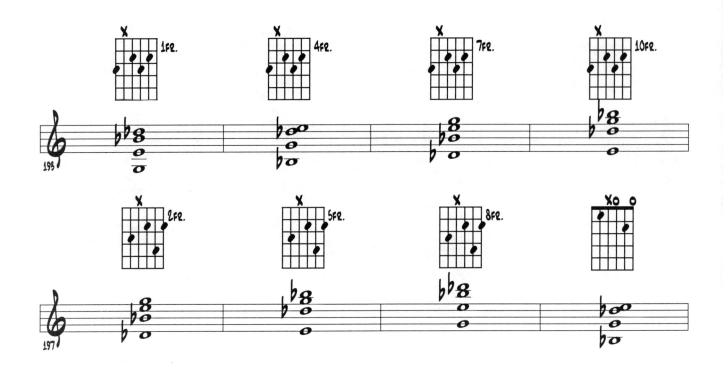

C7(♯9)

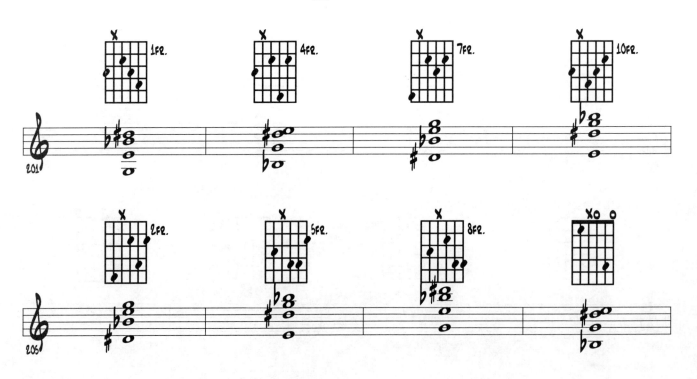

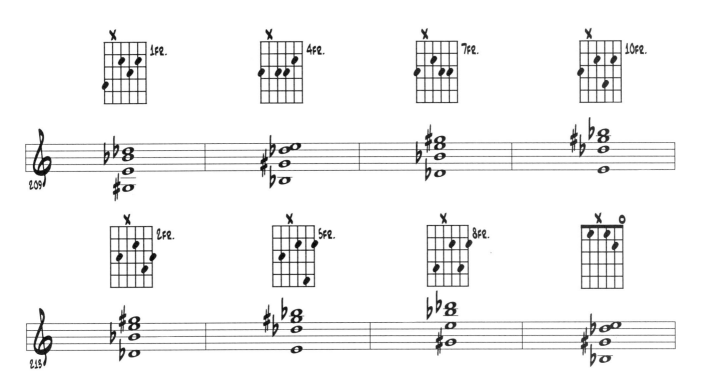

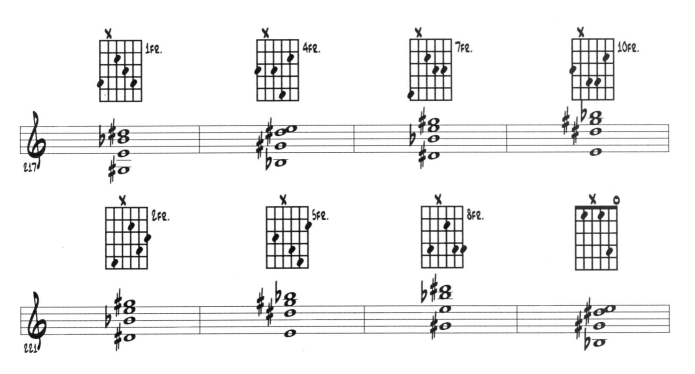

C 13(b9)

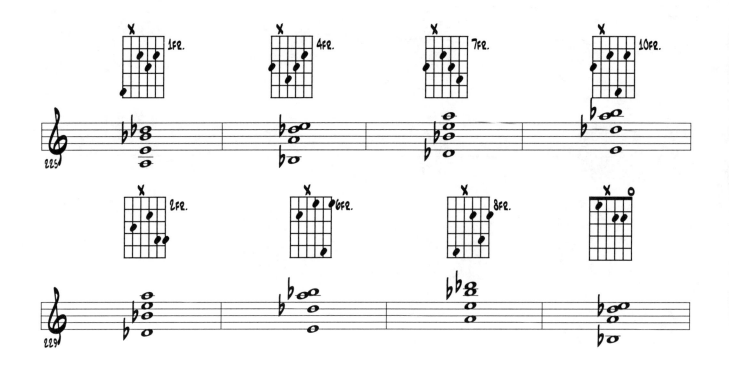

C 13(#9)

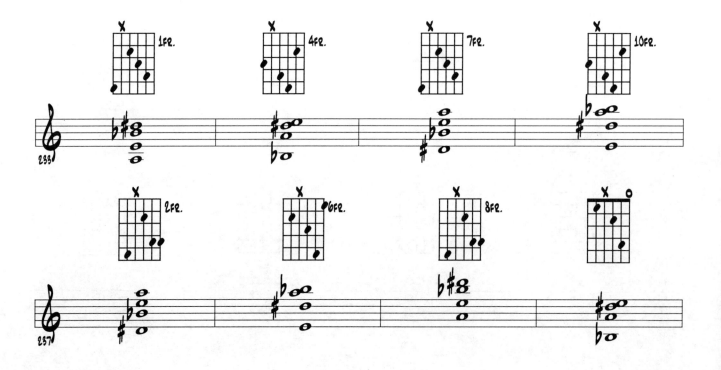

$C7\left(\begin{smallmatrix}b9\\b5\end{smallmatrix}\right)$

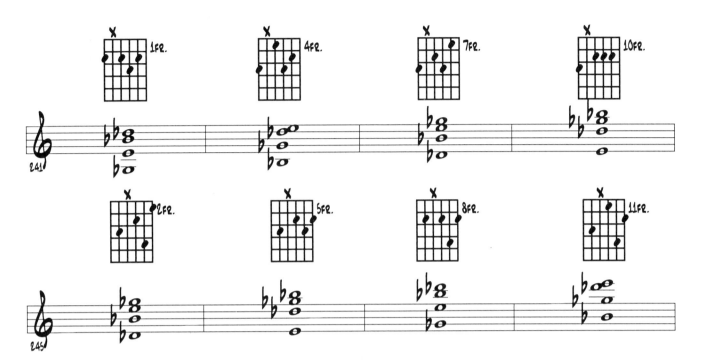

$C7\left(\begin{smallmatrix}\#9\\b5\end{smallmatrix}\right)$

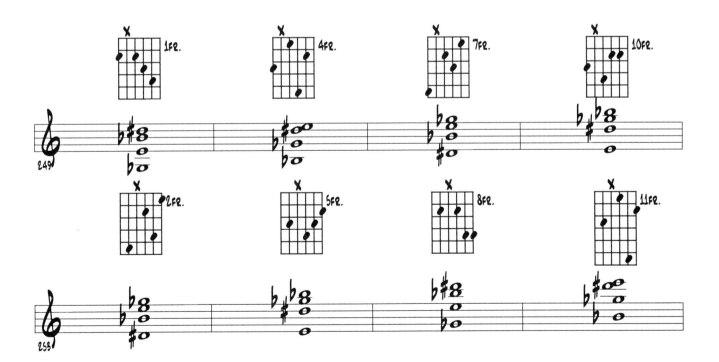

75

C7sus

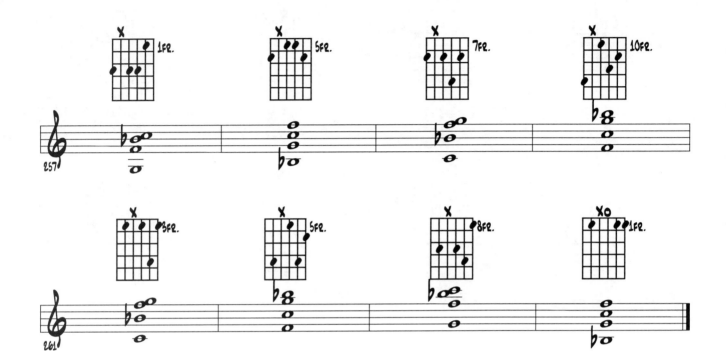

The high density series builds upon the low density series by moving the third note from the bottom up an octave.

Figure 16. High Density Series C△7

Each chord can be played using each of the above voicings on two vertical areas of the neck:

1. lowest note on the sixth string (Bottom Set)

2. lowest note on the fifth string (Top Set)

This results in 12 total chords (4 voicings per veritical area) per chord configuration

5.4.1 Major Chord Family

CΔ7

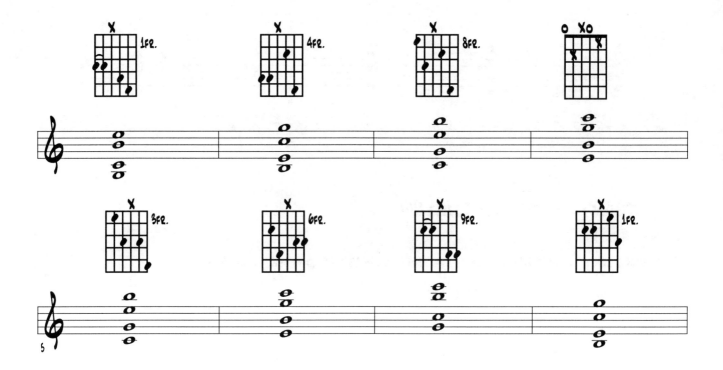

CΔ6

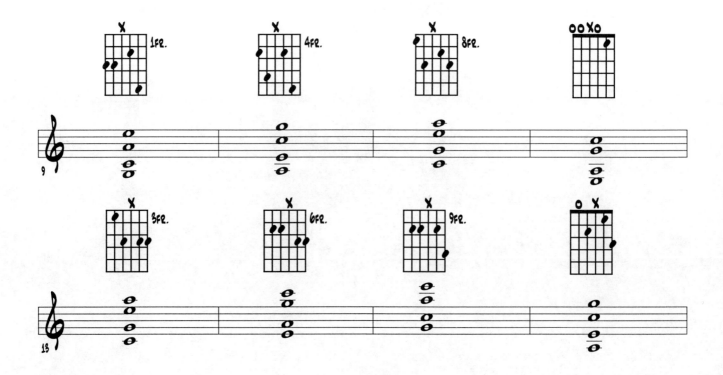

C△7(b5)

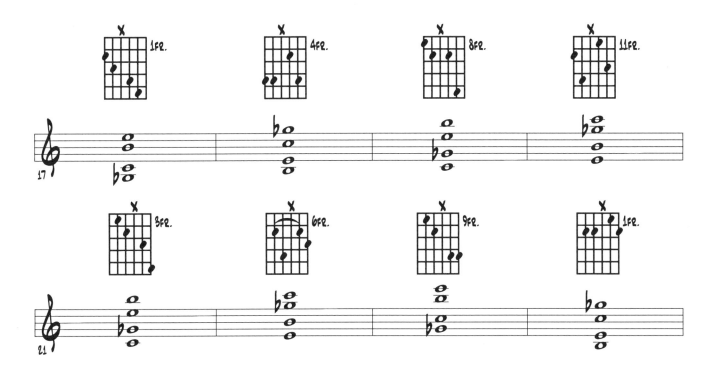

C△add9

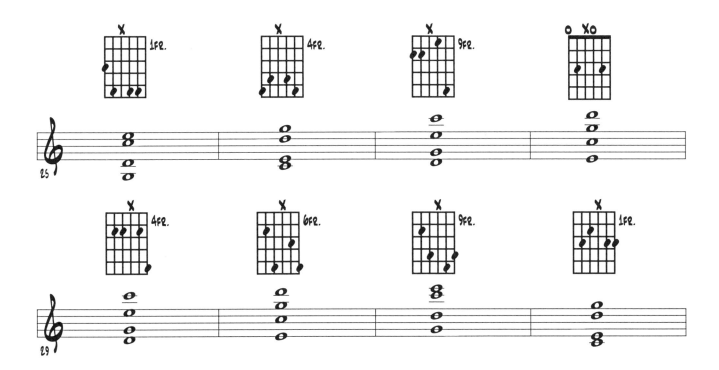

CΔ9

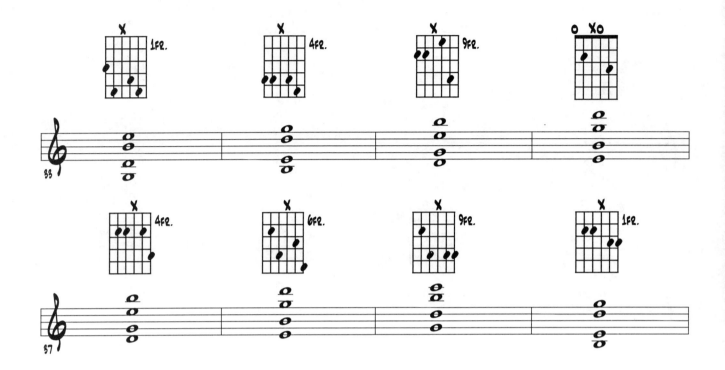

CΔ6/9

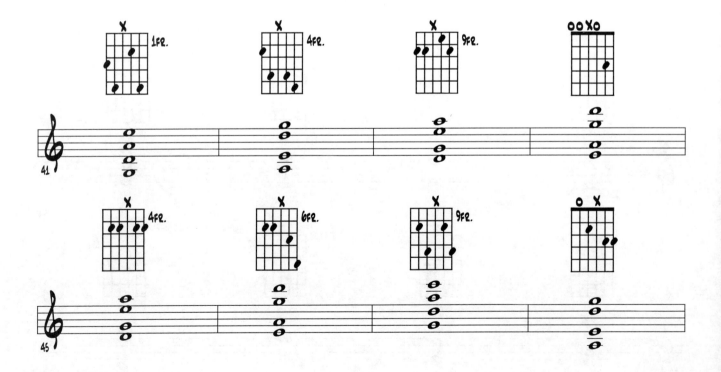

C△7(#5)

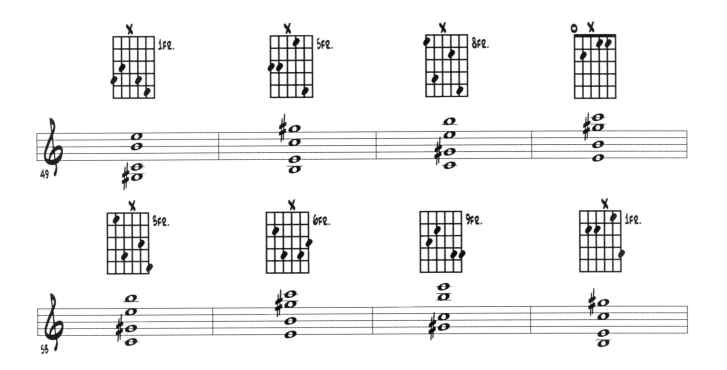

5.4.2 Minor Chord Family

C-7

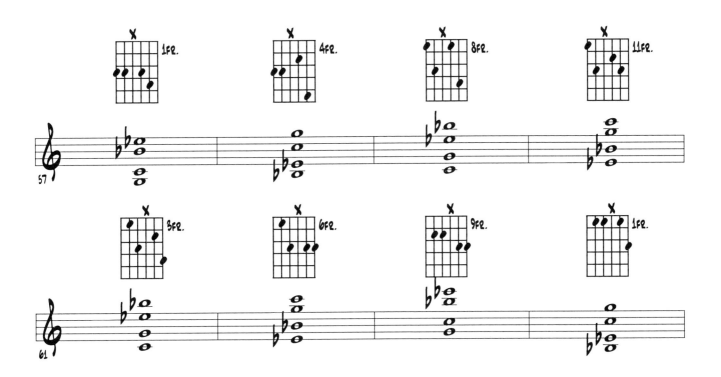

C-6

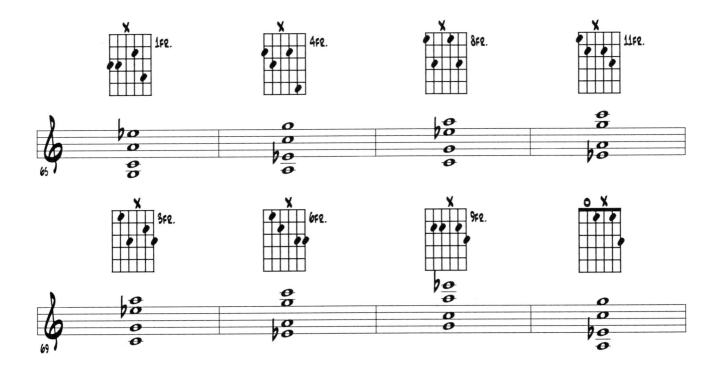

C-7(b5)

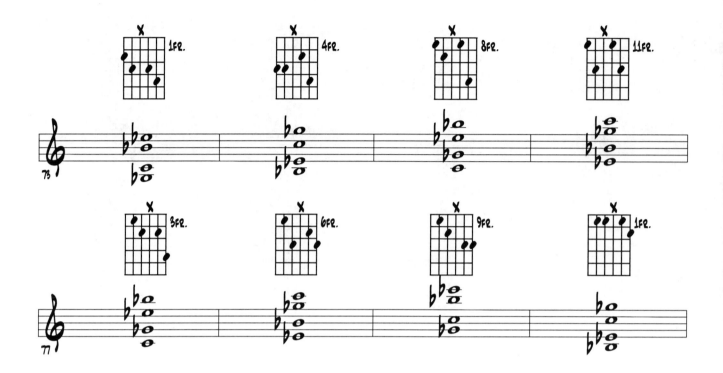

C-ADD9

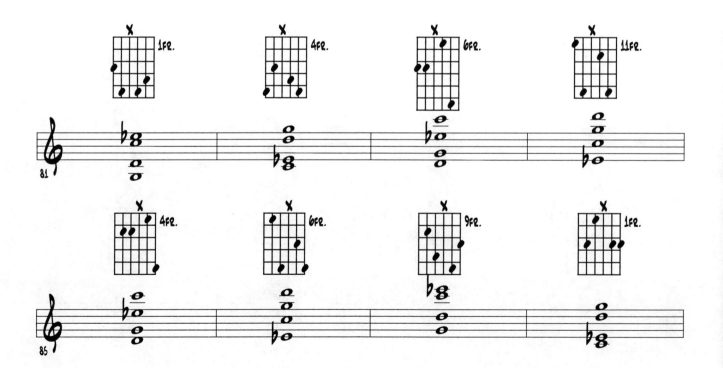

C-9

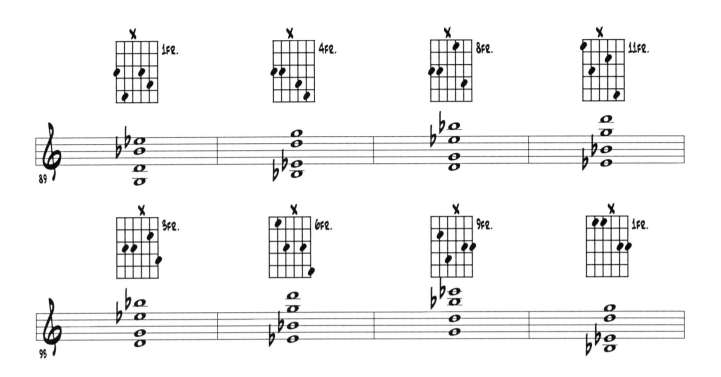

C-(Δ7)

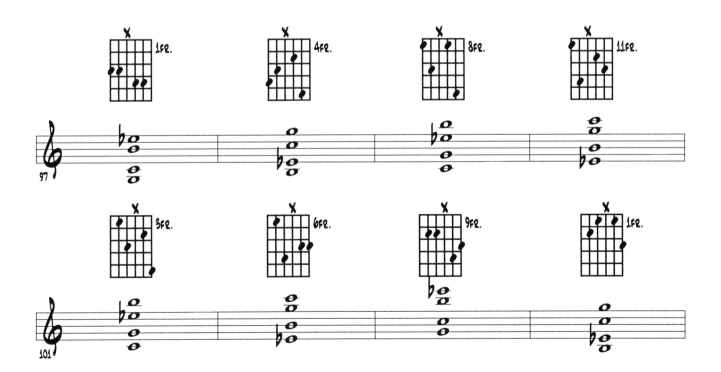

85

C-9(Δ7)

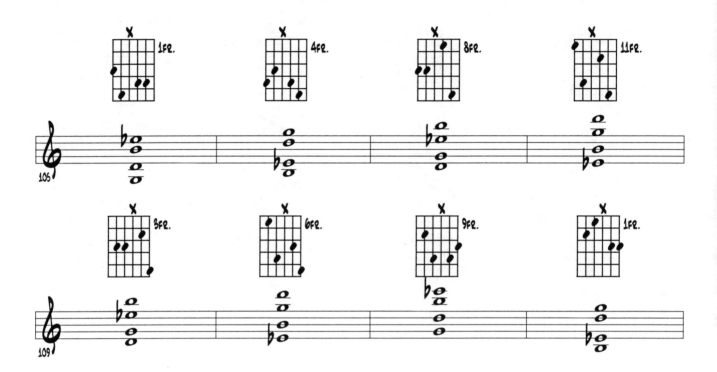

C-9(b5)

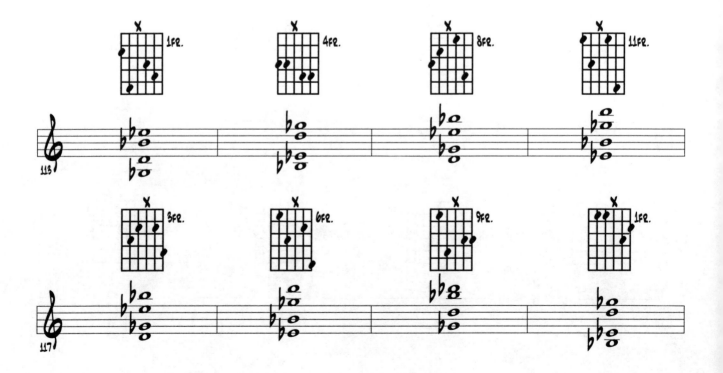

C-6/9

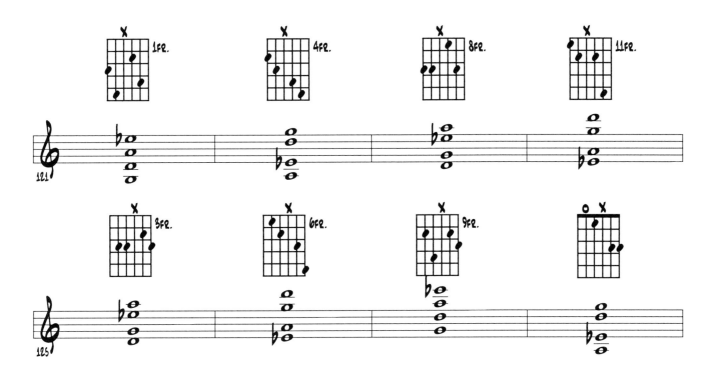

5.4.3 Dominant Chord Family

C7

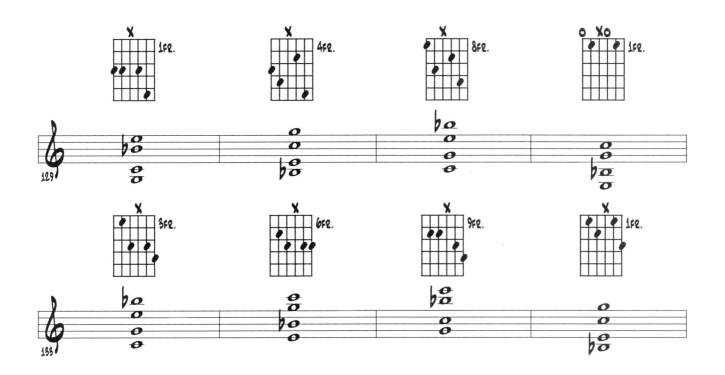

C7(b5)

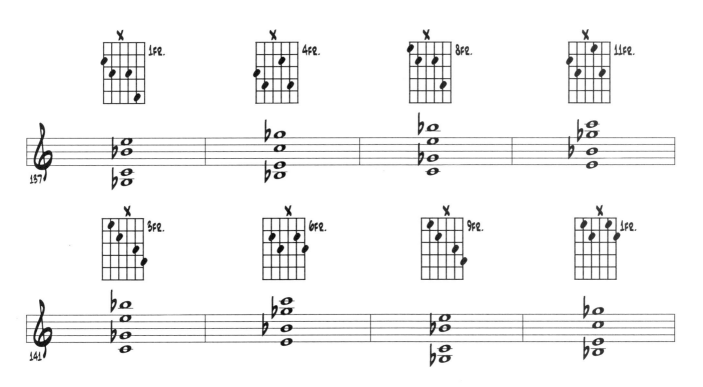

89

C7(#5)

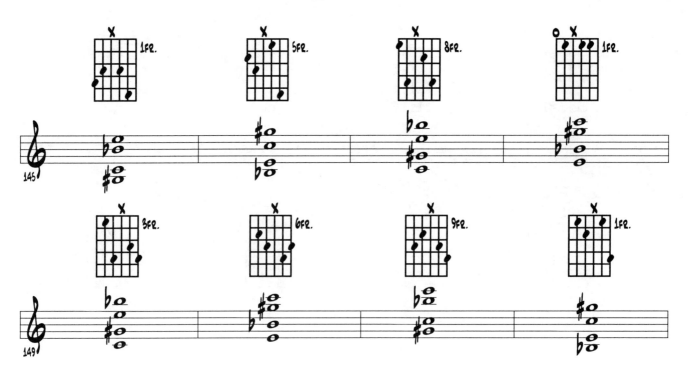

C9

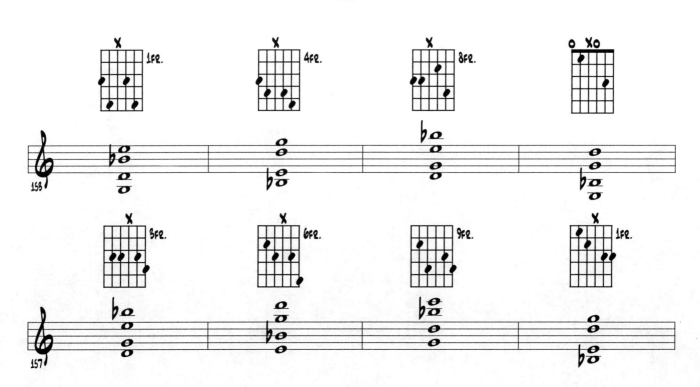

C9(b5)

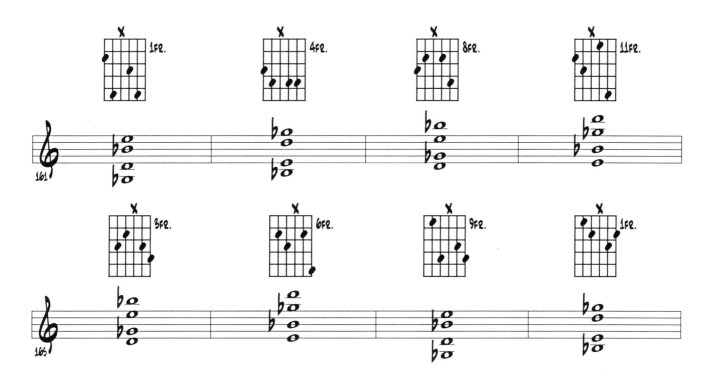

C9(#5)

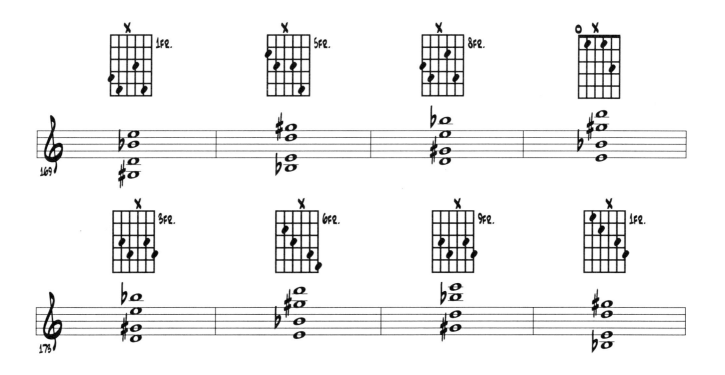

C13

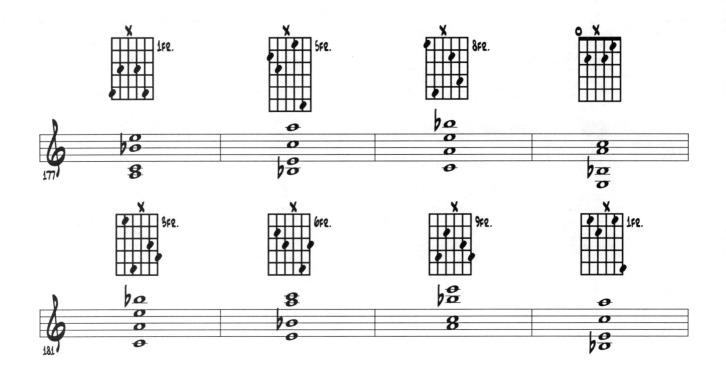

C13ADD9

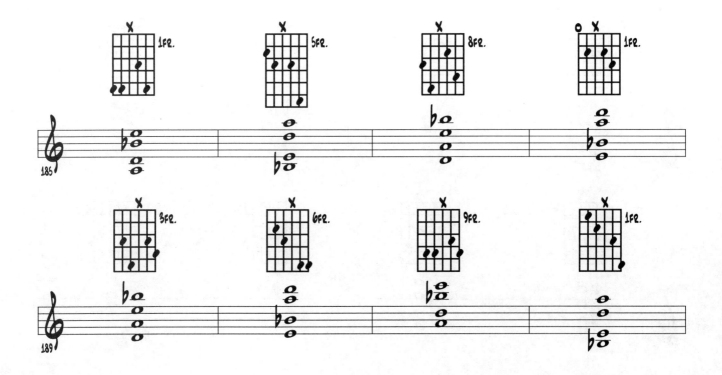

C7(b9)

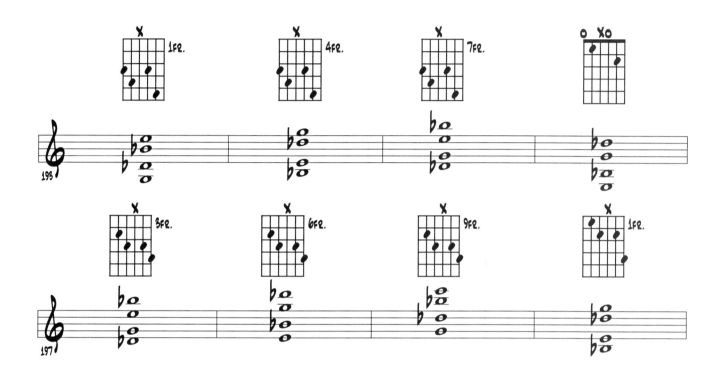

C7(#9)

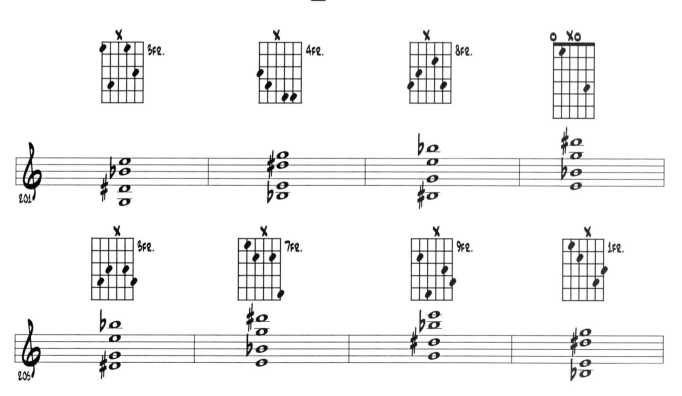

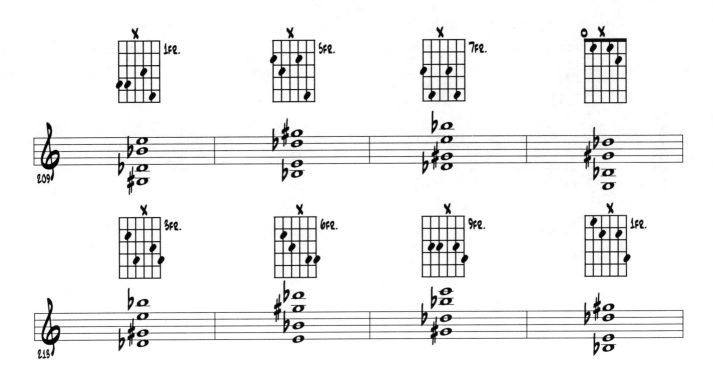

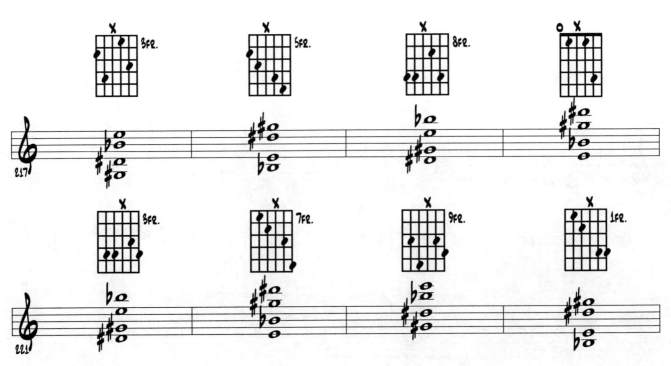

C 13(♭9)

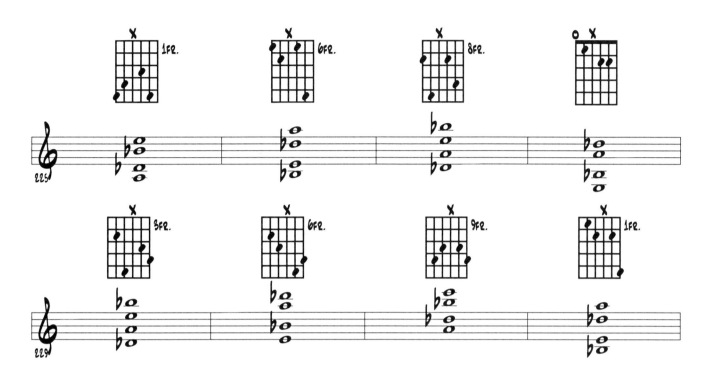

C 13(♯9)

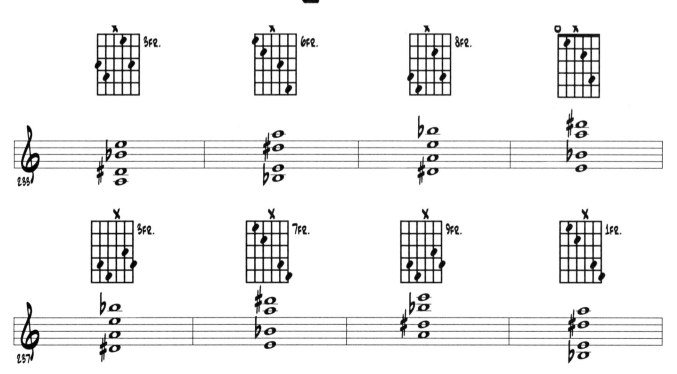

95

C7(♭9 ♭5)

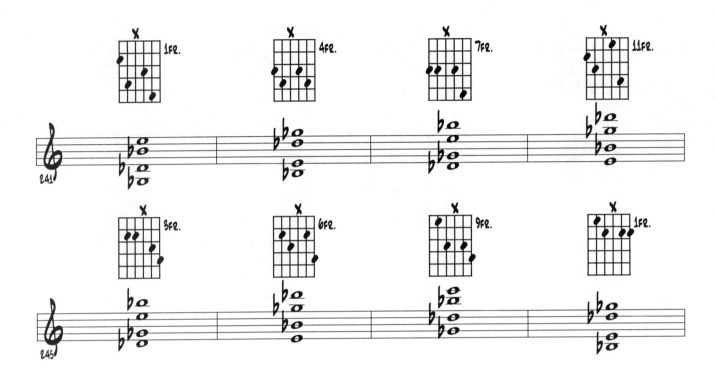

C7(♯9 ♭5)

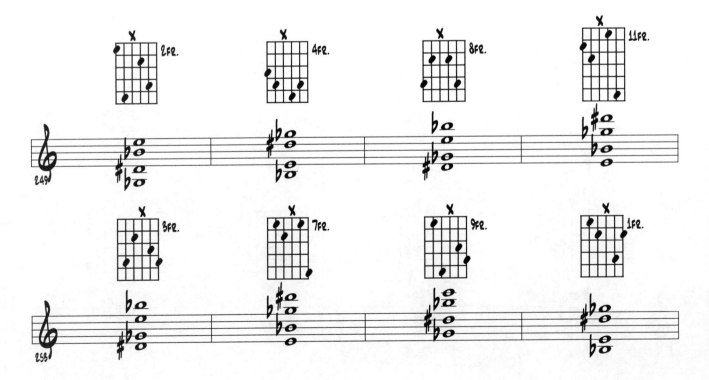

C7sus

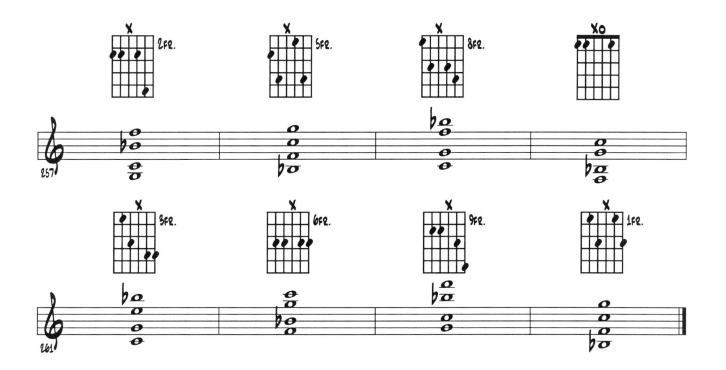

5.5 Cluster Series

The cluster series is a departure from the low, medium, and high density series.

Figure 17. Cluster Series C△7

Cluster series chords can be played on three vertical areas of the neck:

    1. lowest note on the sixth string (Bottom Set)

    2. lowest note on the fifth string (Middle Set)

    3. lowest note on the fourth string (Top Set)

Only two chords are viable in the Top Set, reflected on the following page. Also, when extending or altering this series, various voicings are unplayable based on the key, distance between frets, etc.

I leave it to the reader to work through the cluster series voicings in Table 1, Table 2, and Table 3.

C△7

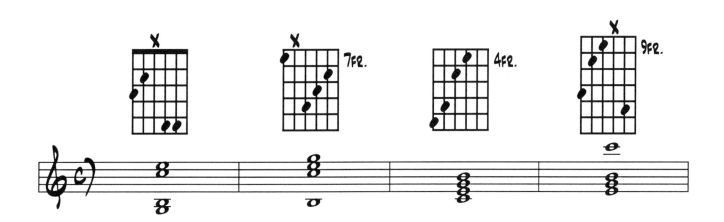

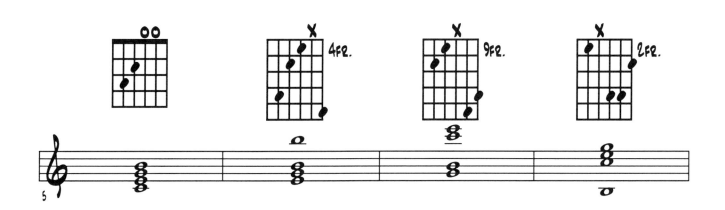

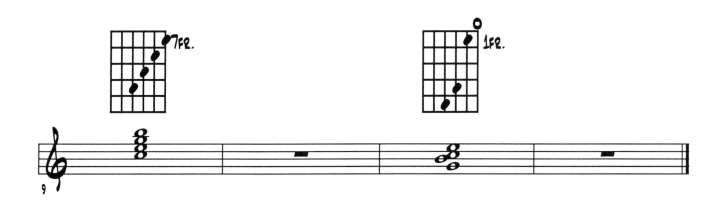

99

5.6 Ninth Series

The ninth series is applicable to only those chords containing a ninth.

Figure 18. C Major 9 (no⁵ᵗʰ) Series

This series has no fifth, which voids voicings with a 5, b5, or #5 in Table 1, Table 2, and Table 3 starting on page 13. Yet, they can be useful in many playing situations.

Ninth series chords can be played on three vertical areas of the neck:

    1. Lowest note on the sixth string (Bottom Set)

    2. Lowest note on the fifth string (Middle Set)

    3. Lowest not on the fourth string (Top Set)

Again, I leave it to the reader to work the ninth series through the individual voicings in Table 1, Table 2, and Table 3.

CΔ9 (NO 5TH)

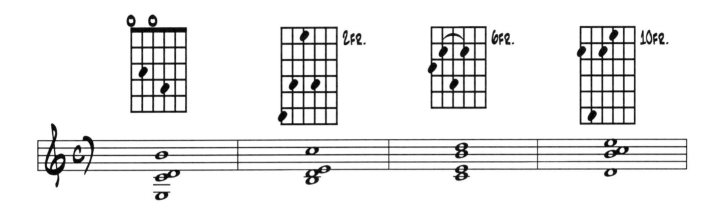

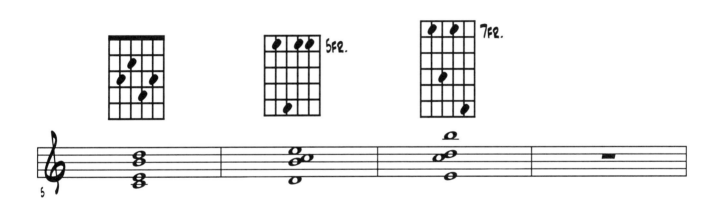

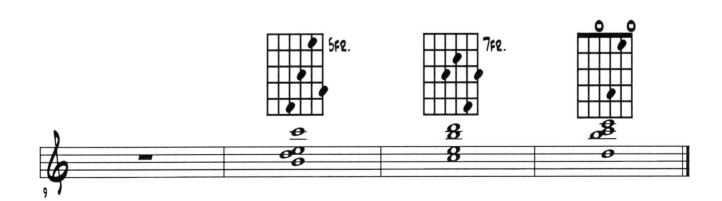

6.0 Practice

6.1 Low Density

One way to practice chord inversions (though you should explore others) is to start with a Low Density Series chord, and walk through all voicings for Major, Minor, and Dominant families. The following pages demonstrate a sample practice session, working through Major voicings in all 12 Low Density chord formations, then performing a similar process for Minor and Dominant chords.

Work on one page a day, and within a year most chords should be within your reach.

6.1.1 Major

The following pages walk through all major family voicings.

BOTTOM SET

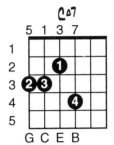
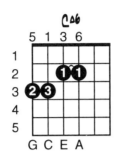
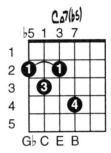
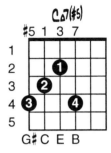

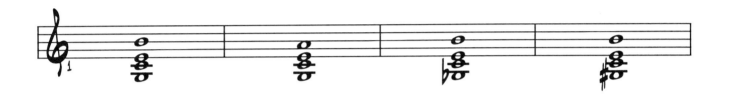

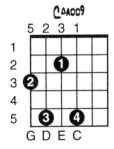
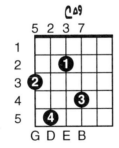
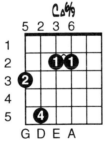

PRACTICE

MAJOR - BOTTOM SET 2

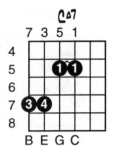

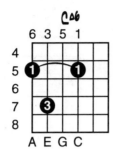

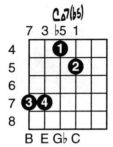

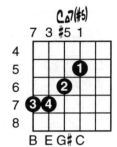

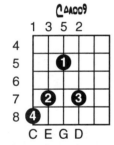

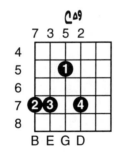

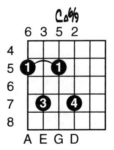

MAJOR – BOTTOM SET 3

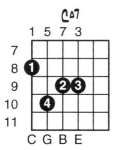

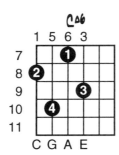

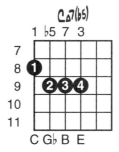

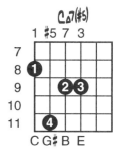

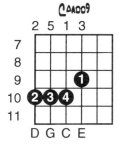

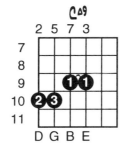

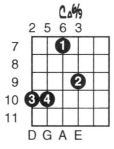

105

MAJOR - BOTTOM SET 4

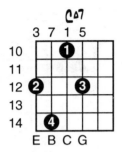

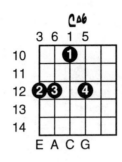

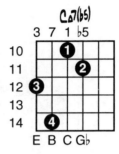

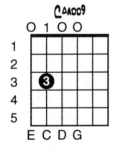

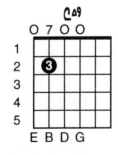

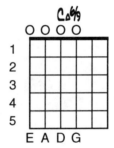

Middle set

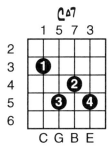

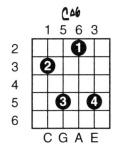

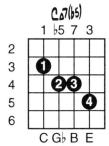

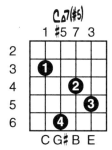

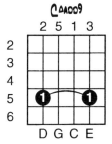

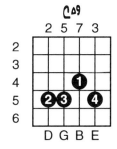

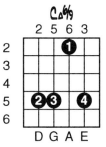

107

MAJOR - MIDDLE SET 2

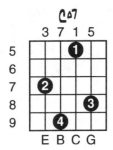

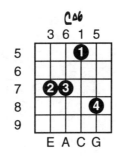

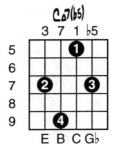

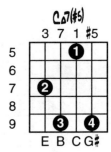

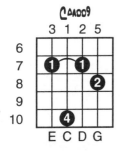

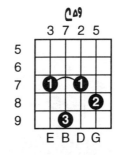

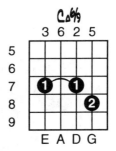

MAJOR - MIDDLE SET 3

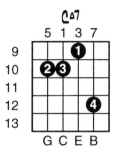

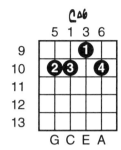

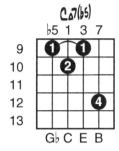

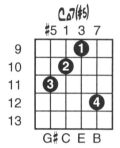

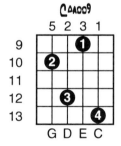

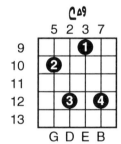

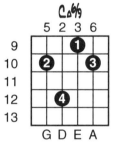

PRACTICE

Major - Middle Set 4

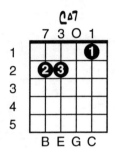

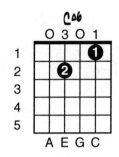

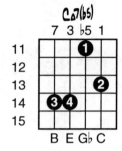

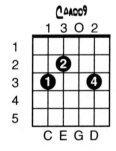

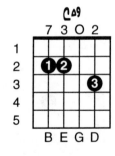

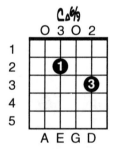

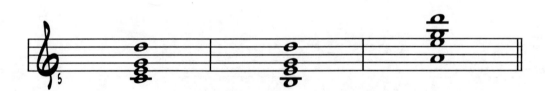

TOP SET

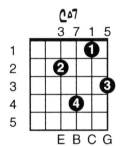

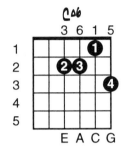

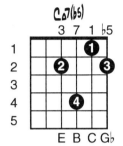

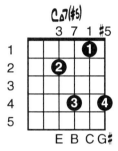

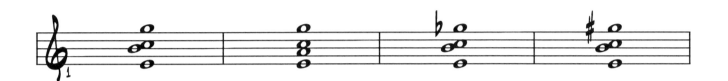

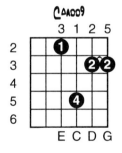

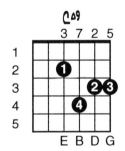

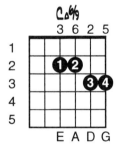

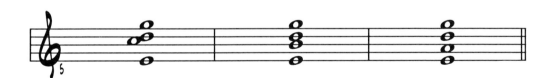

MAJOR - TOP SET 2

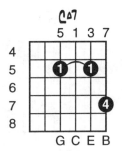

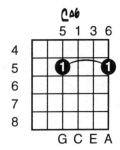

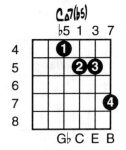

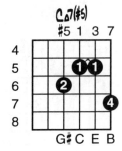

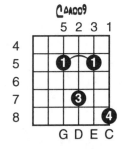

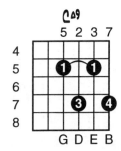

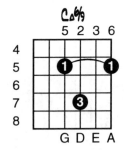

MAJOR – TOP SET 3

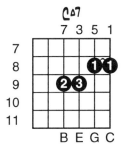

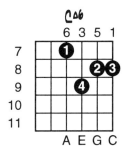

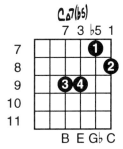

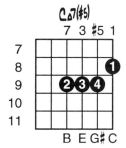

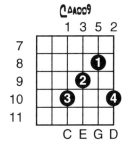

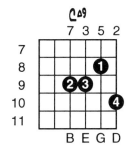

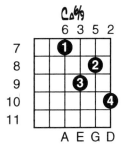

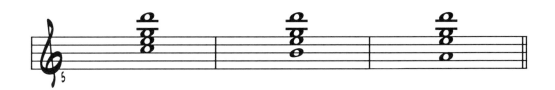

PRACTICE

MAJOR - TOP SET 4

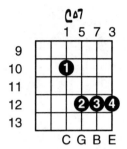

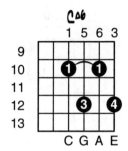

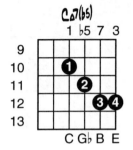

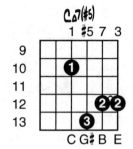

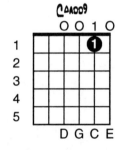

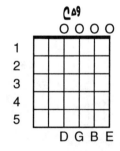

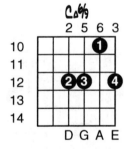

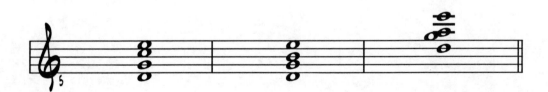

The following pages display all minor family voicings.

Practice

Bottom set

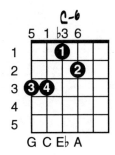

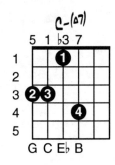

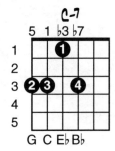

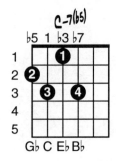

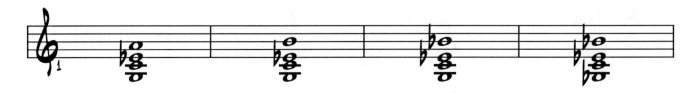

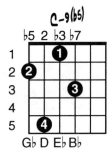

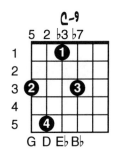

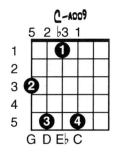

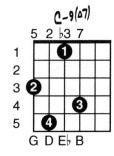

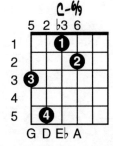

MINOR – BOTTOM SET 2

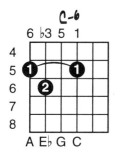

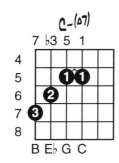

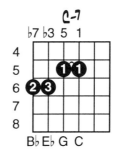

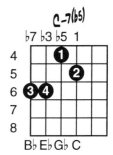

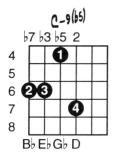

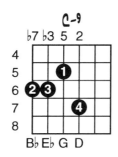

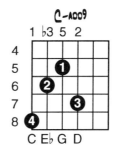

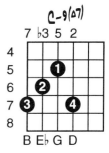

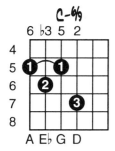

PRACTICE

MINOR – BOTTOM SET 3

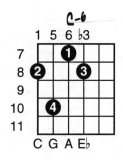
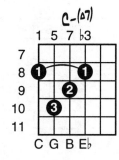
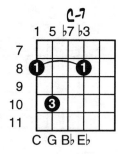
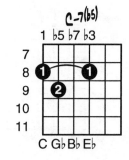

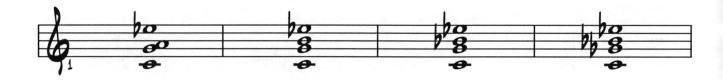

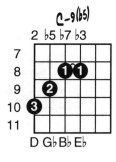
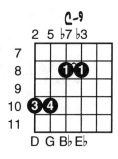
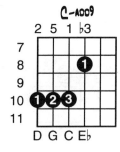
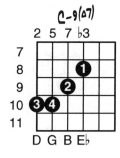

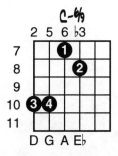

MINOR - BOTTOM SET 4

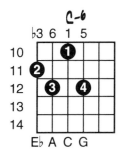

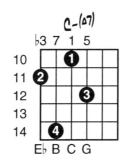

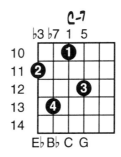

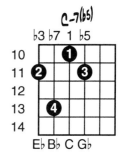

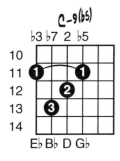

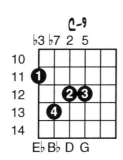

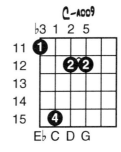

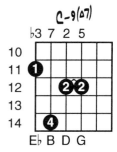

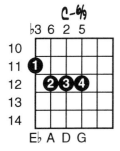

119

MIDDLE SET

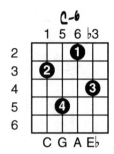
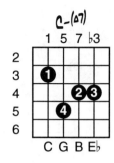
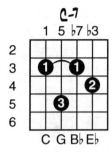

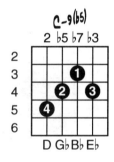
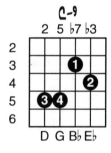
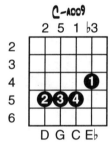
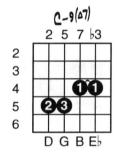

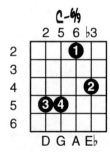

MINOR – MIDDLE SET 2

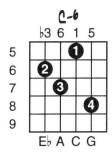

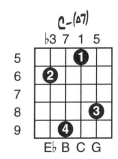

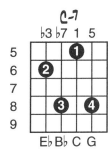

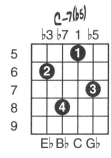

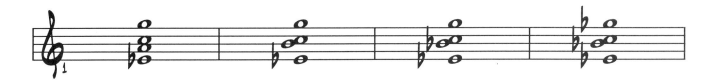

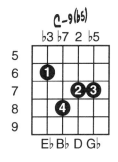

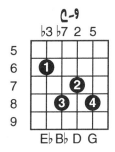

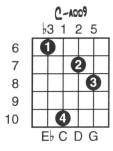

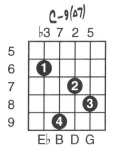

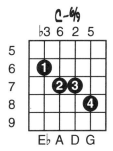

121

MINOR – MIDDLE SET 3

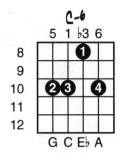

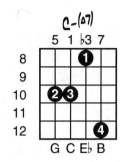

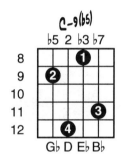

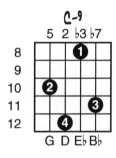

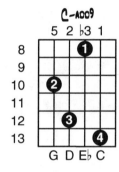

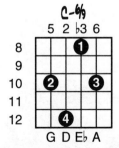

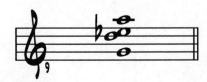

Minor - middle set 4

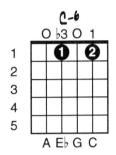

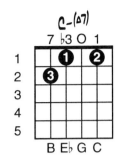

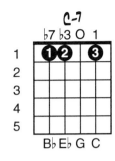

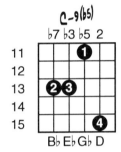

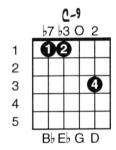

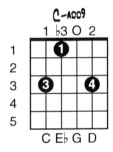

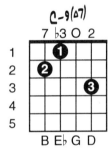

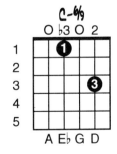

PRACTICE

TOP SET

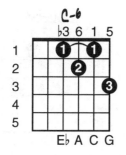

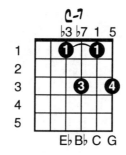

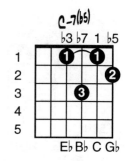

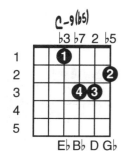

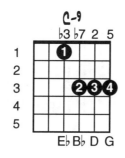

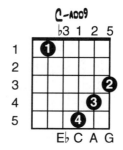

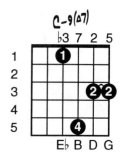

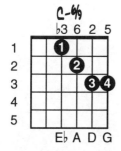

MINOR - TOP SET 2

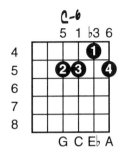

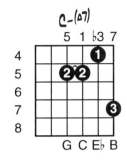

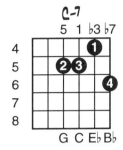

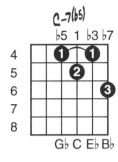

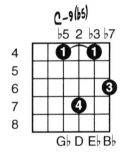

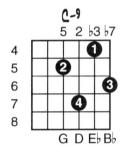

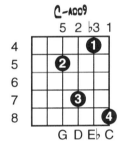

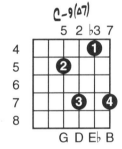

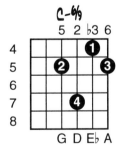

PRACTICE

MINOR – TOP SET 3

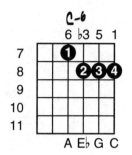

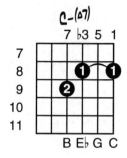

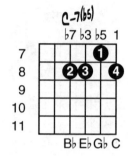

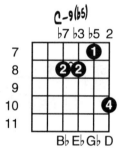

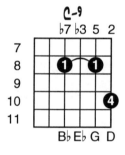

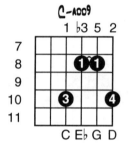

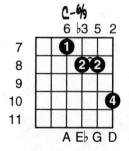

MINOR – TOP SET 4

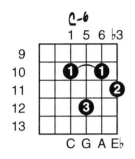
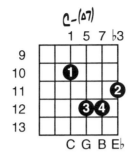
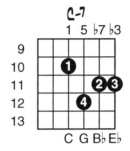

C-6   C-(Δ7)   C-7   C-7(b5)

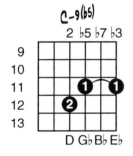
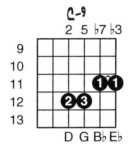
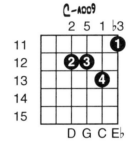

C-9(b5)   C-9   C-ADD9   C-9(Δ7)

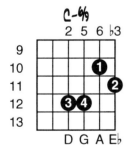

C-6/9

PRACTICE

6.1.3 DOMINANT

The following pages display all dominant family voicings.

Bottom Set

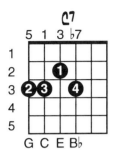 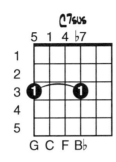 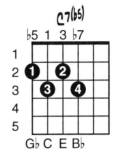 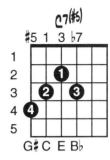

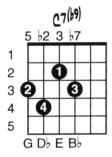 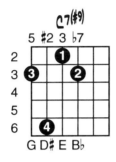 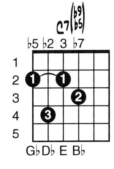 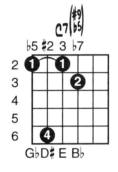

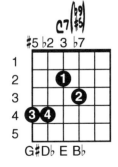 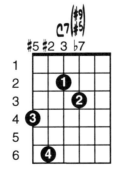 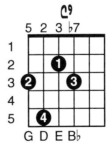 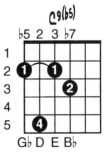

PRACTICE

Dominant – Bottom set 1 (cont.)

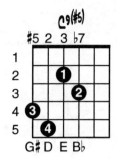

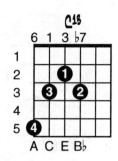

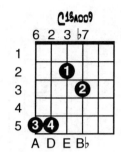

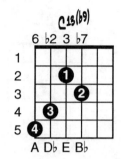

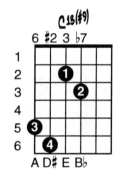

DOMINANT – BOTTOM SET 2

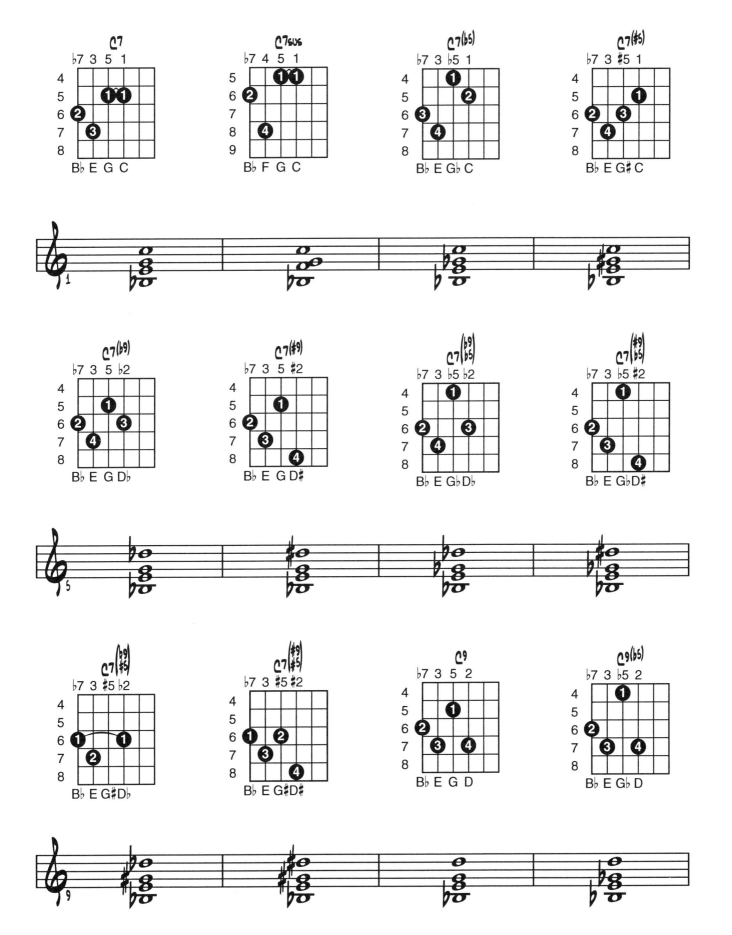

Dominant – Bottom set 2 (cont.)

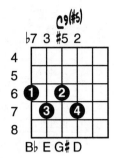

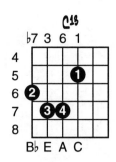

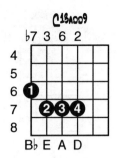

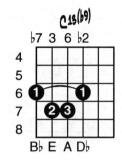

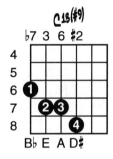

Dominant - Bottom set 3

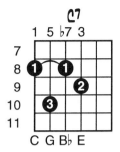
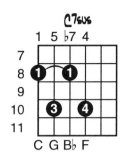
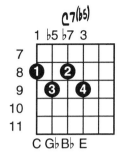
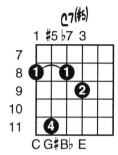

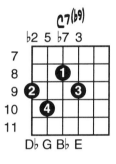
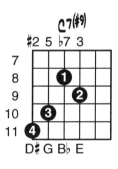
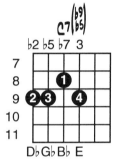
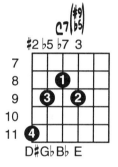

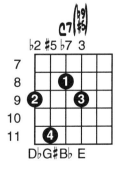
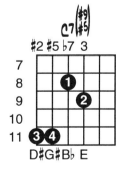
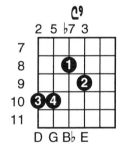
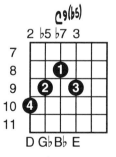

PRACTICE

DOMINANT – BOTTOM SET 3 (CONT.)

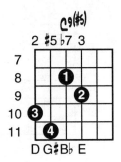
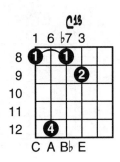
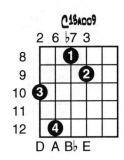

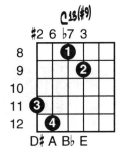

DOMINANT - BOTTOM SET 4

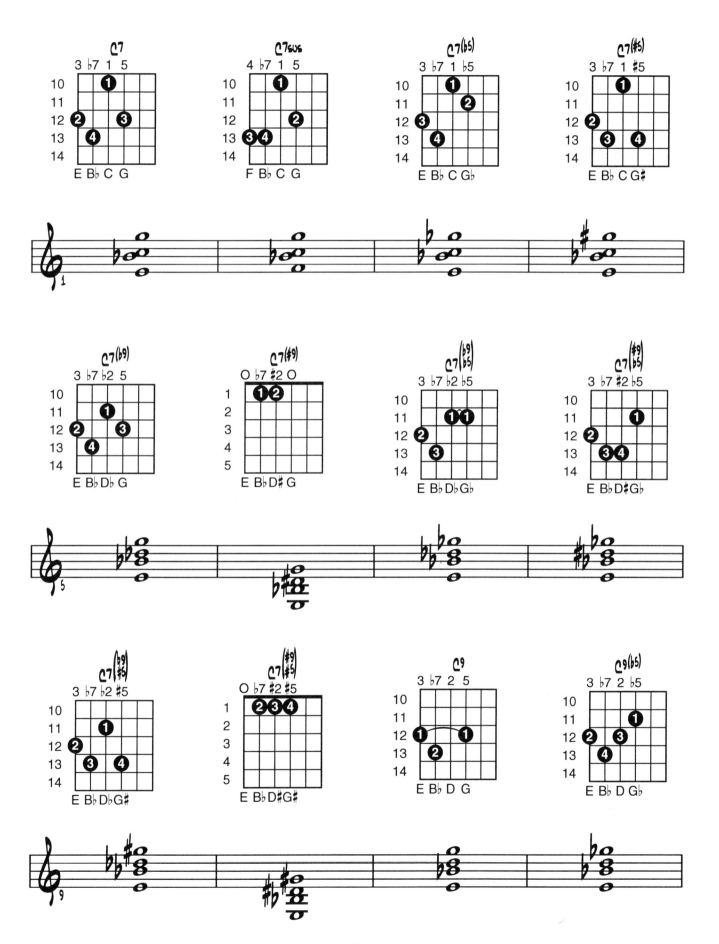

Dominant - Bottom set 4 (cont.)

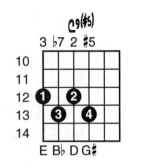

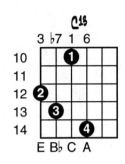

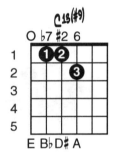

MIDDLE SET

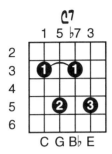

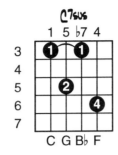

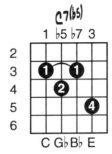

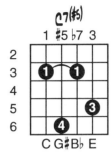

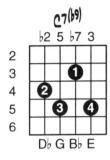

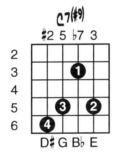

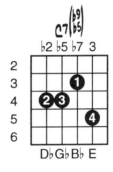

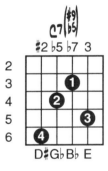

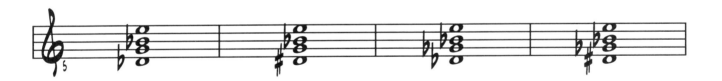

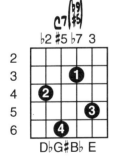

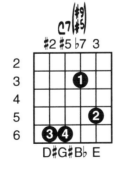

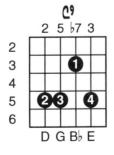

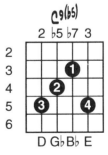

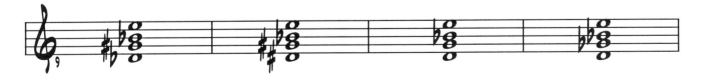

DOMINANT – MIDDLE SET 1 (CONT.)

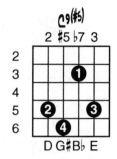

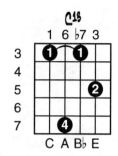

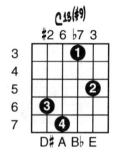

DOMINANT - MIDDLE SET 2

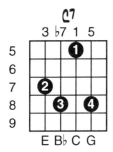

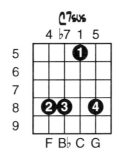

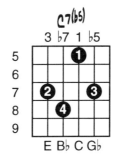

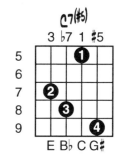

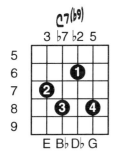

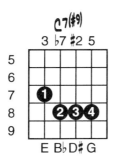

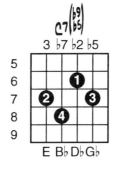

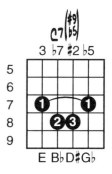

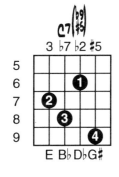

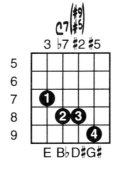

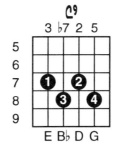

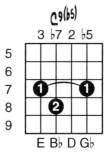

PRACTICE

DOMINANT - MIDDLE SET 2 (CONT.)

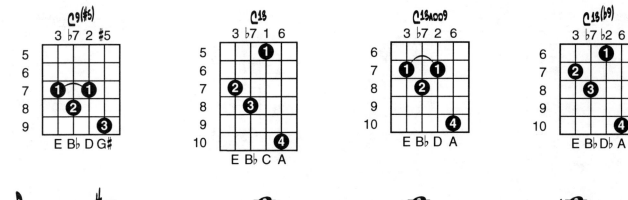

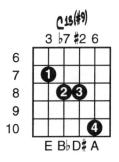

DOMINANT - MIDDLE SET 3

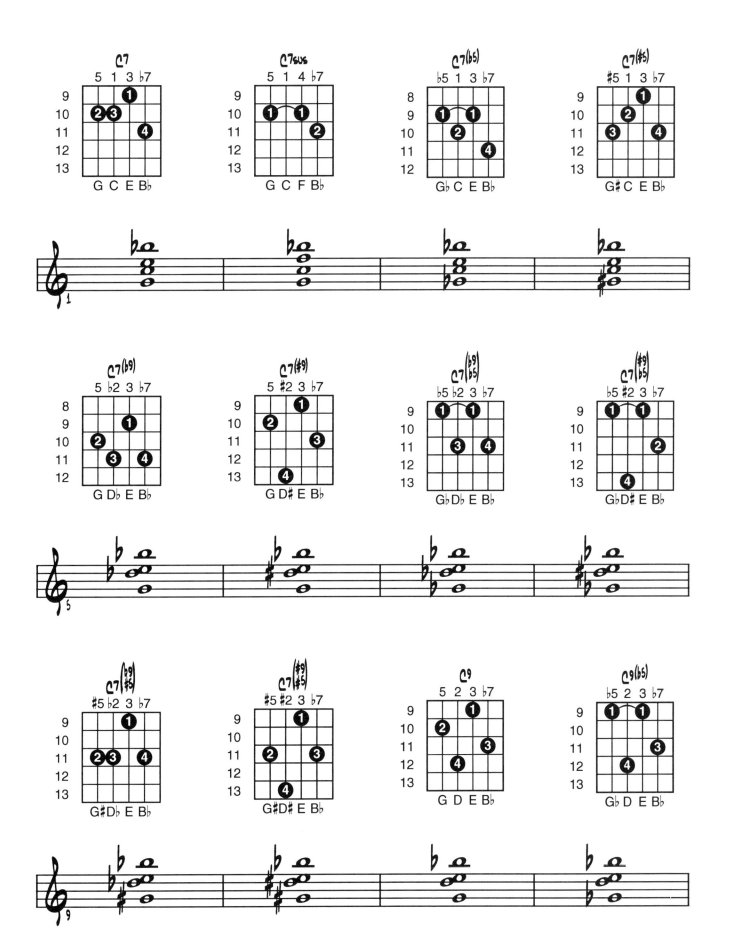

141

DOMINANT - MIDDLE SET 3 (CONT.)

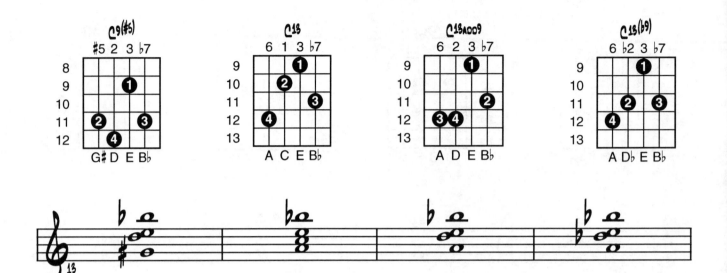

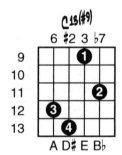

Dominant - middle set 4

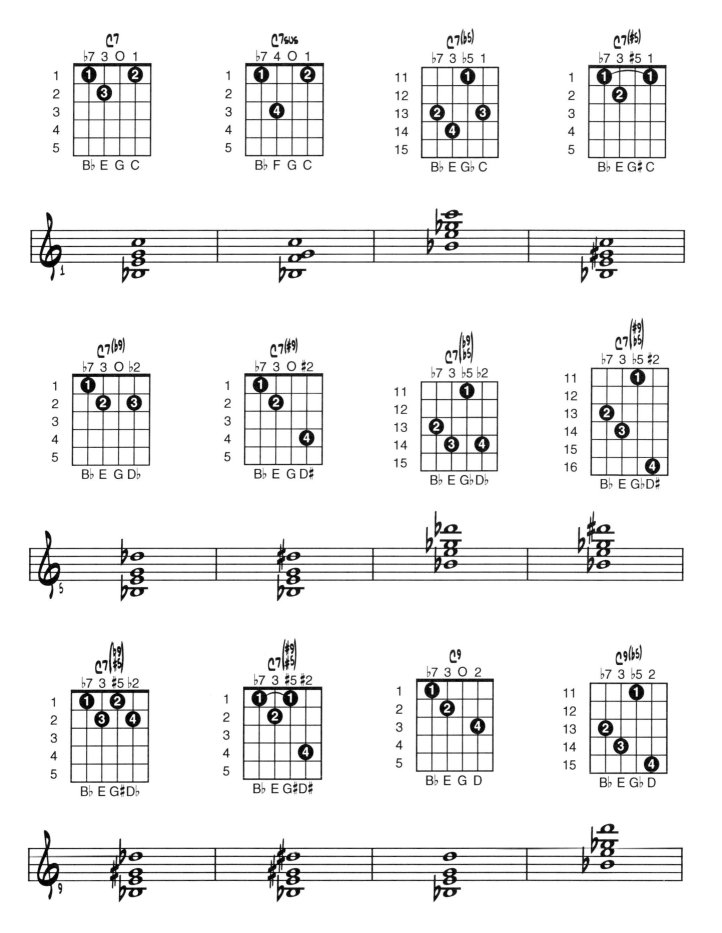

DOMINANT - MIDDLE SET 4 (CONT.)

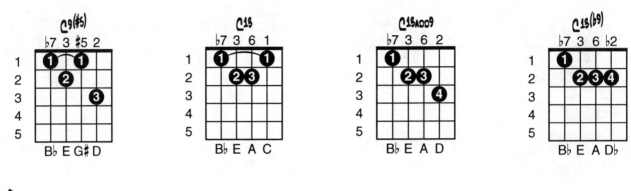

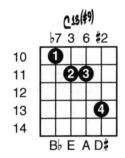

TOP SET

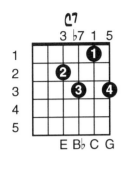

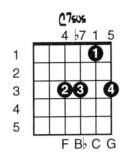

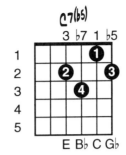

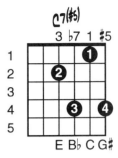

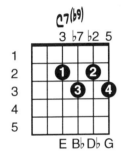

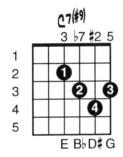

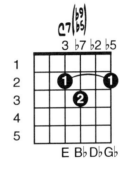

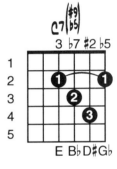

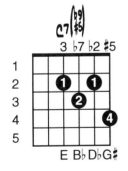

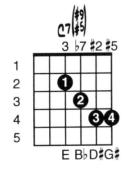

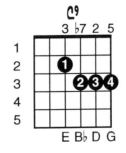

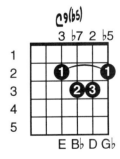

PRACTICE

DOMINANT – TOP SET 1 (CONT.)

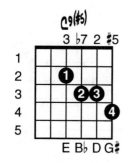

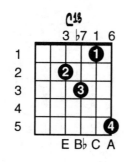

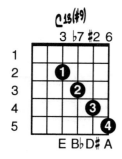

DOMINANT – TOP SET 2

PRACTICE

DOMINANT – TOP SET 2 (CONT.)

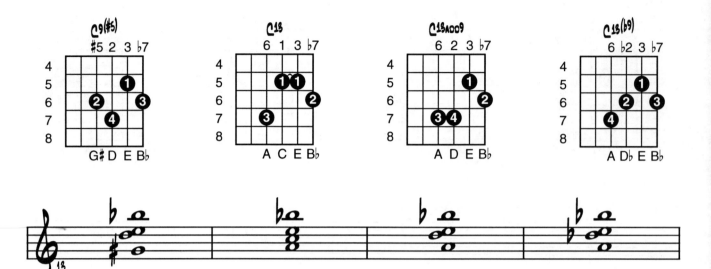

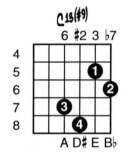

DOMINANT - TOP SET 3

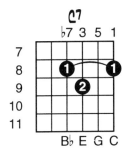

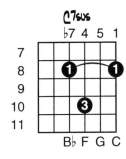

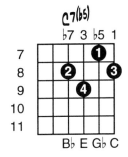

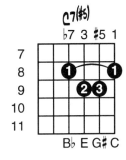

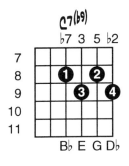

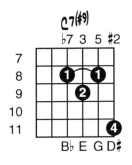

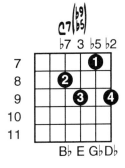

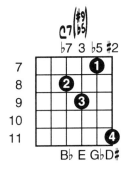

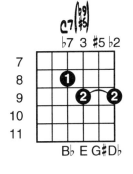

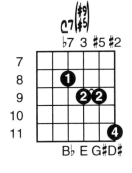

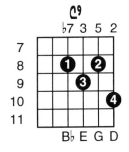

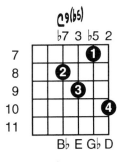

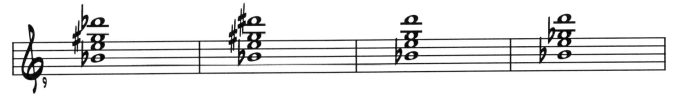

PRACTICE

DOMINANT - TOP SET 3 (CONT.)

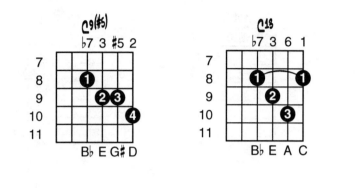

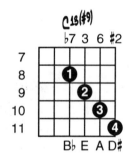

Dominant - top set 4

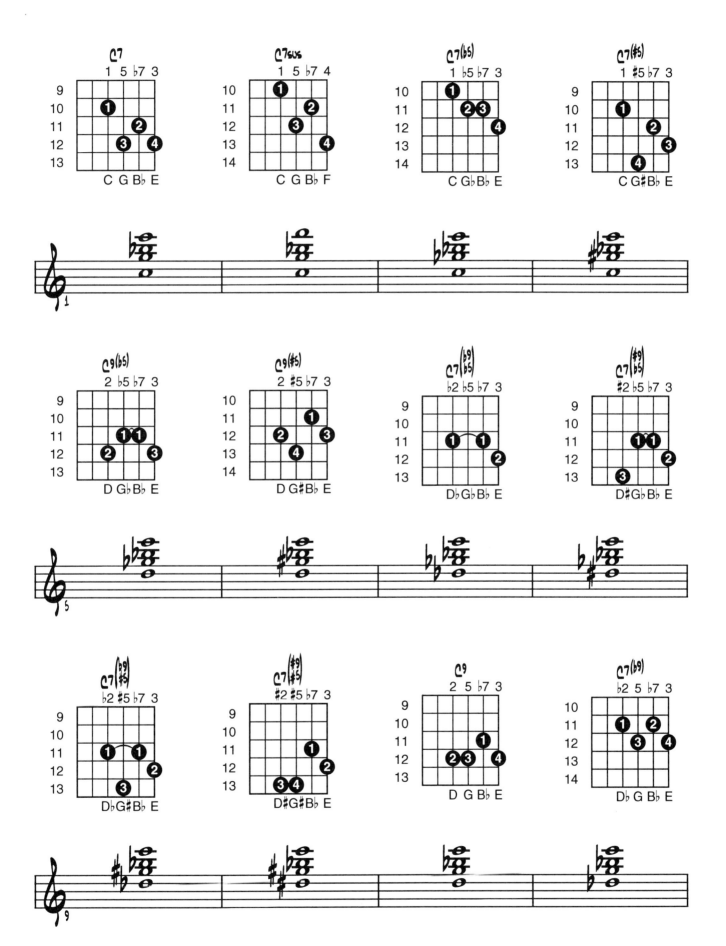

DOMINANT – TOP SET 4 (CONT.)

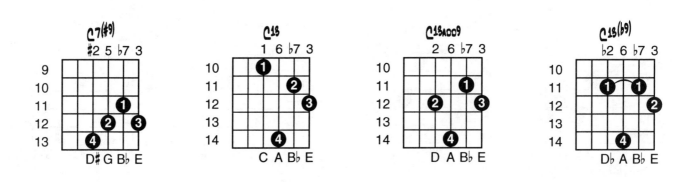

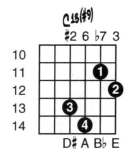

153

Bottom set

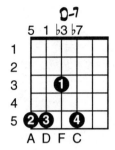

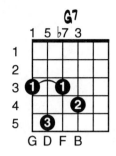

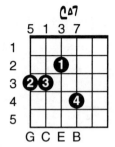

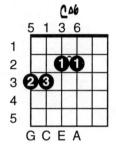

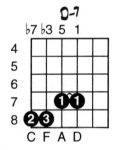

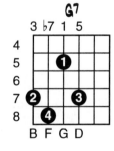

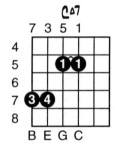

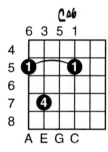

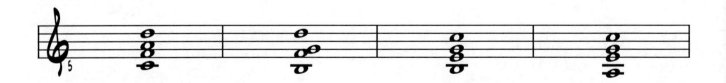

BOTTOM SET (CONT.)

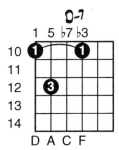

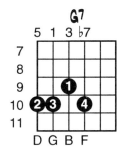

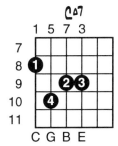

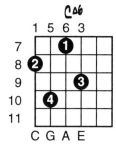

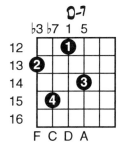

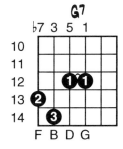

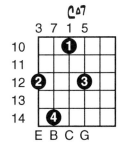

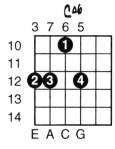

MIDDLE SET

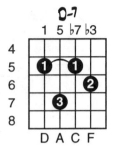

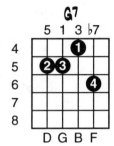

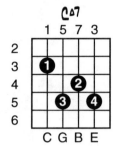

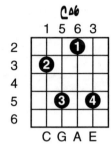

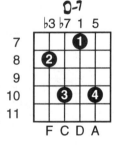

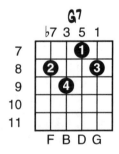

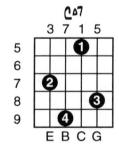

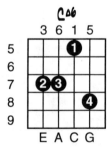

MIDDLE SET (CONT.)

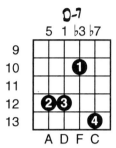
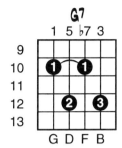
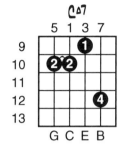
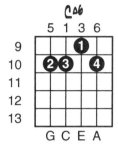

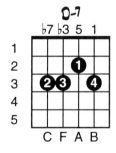
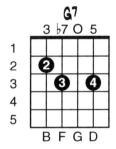
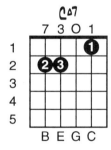

PRACTICE

TOP SET

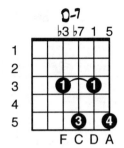
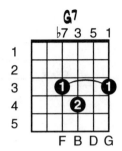
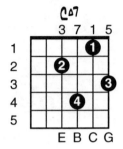
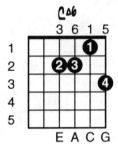

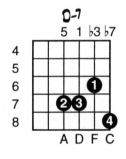
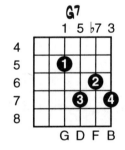
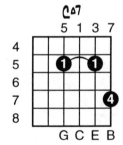
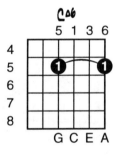

TOP SET (CONT.)

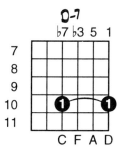
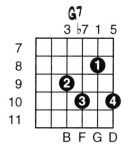
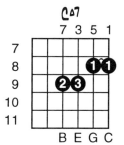
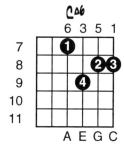

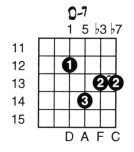
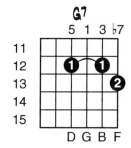
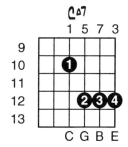
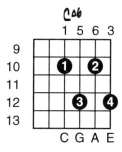

159

6.3 Diatonic Chord Scale

Figure 19 uses a single voicing (fifth, root, third, and seventh in this example) to form a diatonic chord scale. For color, add extensions and alterations to the chords.

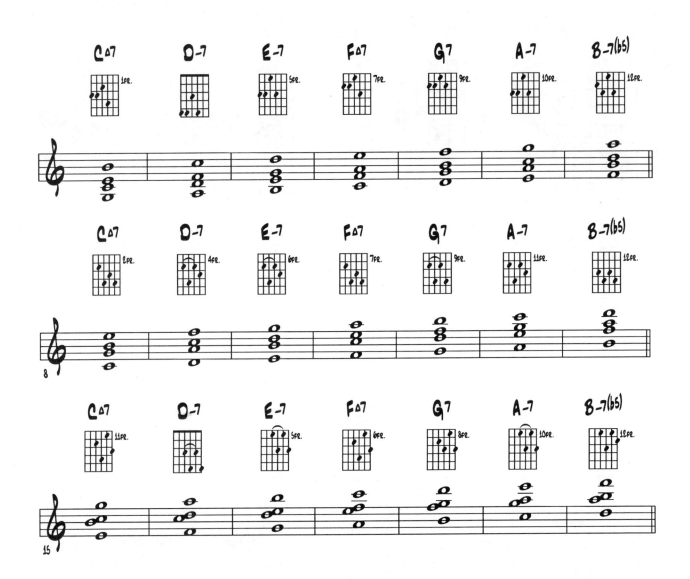

Figure 19. Diatonic Chord Scale